The Scholar Adventurer

◆

The

SCHOLAR

ADVENTURER

A Tribute to John D. Gordan (1907–1968)

on the Eightieth Anniversary

of His Birth

With Six of His Essays

◆

THE NEW YORK PUBLIC LIBRARY

1987

This volume is produced with the assistance of the
Judge and Mrs. Samuel D. Levy Memorial Publication Fund.

Copyright © 1987 The New York Public Library,
Astor, Lenox and Tilden Foundations

Distributed by the Publishing Center for Cultural Resources
Acknowledgments for previously published material will
be found on p. 131–132.

Library of Congress Cataloging-in-Publication Data

Gordan, John Dozier, 1907–1968.
The scholar adventurer: a tribute to John D. Gordan
(1907–1968) on the 80th anniversary of his birth:
with six of his essays. xxiv, 134 pp. 14 x 22.8 cm.
ISBN 0-87104-294-0 (pbk.)
1. Gordan, John Dozier, 1907–1968.
2. Librarians – United States – Biography.
3. Berg Collection.
4. English literature – Library resources – New York (N.Y.)
5. American literature – Library resources – New York (N.Y.)
I. Title.
Z720.G66A3 1987
020'.92'4 – dc19
[B]
87–18136

For his children

Marjorie,

John,

Lucy,

and Virginia

Contents

Foreword

◆

JOHN DOZIER GORDAN, VIRGINIAN, was almost born in Cuba. He often recounted a version of his story about how his mother, approaching her term of pregnancy, was caught in a hurricane while traveling and was nearly dispatched to Cuba. Had that been the case, his entire life might have taken a different, if no less adventurous, turn. The way it did turn out made a world of difference to all of us who knew him. He was born in Norfolk, Virginia, on November 11, 1907. He went to Harvard where he received a B.A. in 1930 and a Ph.D. in English literature in 1939. From 1930 to 1939 he also taught there, and counted among his students such distinguished men as Leonard Bernstein. In World War II he served as a Lieutenant Commander in the Navy, but we remember him best as the indefatigable, colorful, handsome, humorous, and agile Curator of the Henry W. and Albert A. Berg Collection of English and American Literature, a post he held from 1940 until his death in 1968.

He was among the first serious critics and lifelong admirers of Joseph Conrad. His thesis, *Joseph Conrad: The Making of a Novelist*, published in book form by Harvard University Press in 1940, became one of the cornerstones of

Conrad studies. In 1939 John Gordan and his bride, Phyllis Goodhart Gordan, had made the journey to Borneo to gather material about the little native state Conrad called Sambir in *Almayer's Folly* and *An Outcast of the Islands*. His last journeys, because the scholar adventurer never tired, were to England and the Caribbean in search of Elinor Wylie's last romantic attachment. Between those two trips there were countless others: to England, to the Continent, to Greece, to Italy, and to Egypt. Not only did he act as tireless acquisitor for the Berg Collection – he was also this institution's best ambassador.

His primary scholarly and social – one could almost say personal – devotion was to the Berg Collection. Dr. Albert A. Berg and John D. Gordan arrived at The New York Public Library at around the same time. In 1939, when the donor was looking for a librarian, he was fortunate in finding just the right sort of young man. John Gordan first had to learn what technical processes the Library used, and he spent time in Cataloging. He then took a short course at the Main Reference Desk. By the time Dr. Berg's collection increased ten-fold, John Gordan also knew the wider shores of the book world, and wrote the first scholarly piece about its enrichment. The Berg Collection was competitive in its holdings of Charles Dickens with such venerable institutions as the British Museum and the Victoria and Albert Museum, beneficiaries of Dickens' papers after his death. John Gordan devoted his opening exhibition in 1941 to the great English novelist. Thirty-seven similar exhibitions followed during his twenty-eight-year tenure in the Library: tributes to Thackeray, Dr. Berg's other great nineteenth-century author, Wordsworth, George Gissing, and Arnold Bennett marked milestones in English literature. With Walt Whitman, Hawthorne, and Carl Van Vechten he peppered the history of American letters. *Landmarks of English Literature, Novels in Manuscript*, and *Doctors as Men of Letters* testify to the breadth of John Gordan's knowledge, and his exhibition of pseudonymous authors reflected the ever-present playfulness of his unique character. The new acquisitions exhibitions were a powerful education to institutional and private collectors, and an English friend wrote of the scholar adventurer: "The rich booming voice and the quick, sure steps that heralded his arrival were very welcome sounds in London, just as they were in New York." His charm blended with scepticism, his brilliant mind observed and imposed high standards both in scholarship and in manner.

John Gordan took on heavy responsibilities outside his regular duties: he never missed a directors' meeting of the Keats-Shelley Association of America or the Bibliographical Society, of which he was president for a term in the mid-1950s. The dapper young man, whose musical ear prompted him to sing popular musicals during office hours, was to be seen at the Boston Symphony and the Metropolitan Opera, both lifelong devotions. In June 1938, while researching his book on Joseph Conrad, John Gordan married his perfect partner, Phyllis Goodhart Gordan, Renaissance scholar and editor of the letters of Poggio Bracciolini. Four children provided enrichment and, surely, entertainment and concern: one of them, when visiting his father on Saturdays, would find him crouching under the Berg readers' table playing hide-and-seek! Recipients of John Gordan's affection took in a world of friendship. Those who were hospitalized, or whose relatives were ill, could look for a daily visitor, and the mother of at least one was buried by him. One could say that he ran a travel agency for those about to go abroad, a literary agency for those who were on the point of getting into print, a theatrical agency for would-be actors. He came forward with brokerage advice, real estate opinion, and, always, advice about the ways of scholarship.

John Gordan also had a remarkable memory – universal, it seemed, unlimited. A melody or a quotation would come to his mind in seconds, and he did not need a catalogue to remember authors and titles. He was always conscious of time. Not necessarily of "Time's wingèd chariot," but its good use. His punctuality was almost pedantic; but, in another way, time's passing in important dates, like publication dates, birthdays, death dates, left its own trail. In managerial time-motion studies John Gordan would never have missed a quickstep, and his tall walk was that of a born dancer. We are marking his eightieth birthday not because he would have expected it, but because those of us who knew him, either fleetingly or well, cannot let it pass unnoticed.

LOLA L. SZLADITS
Curator, Berg Collection

November 11, 1987

The Search for Sambir

---

by Richard D. Altick

◆

To tell the truth, men and women incurably afflicted with wanderlust could hardly choose a more agreeable profession than literary scholarship. Given a suitable research project, and the necessary time and money, they would have a perfect rationalization for their itching feet. The history of modern scholarship has plenty of distinguished precedents. In gathering the materials for her exhaustive study of the antecedents of the Barrett and Browning families, Jeannette Marks lived for months in the West Indies. One summer during the 1930s, Howard F. Lowry and Chauncey Brewster Tinker devoted their holiday to traveling to Switzerland in the hope of finding a clue to the mysterious girl who, eighty years earlier, charmed the youthful Matthew Arnold and became the "Marguerite" of some of his best-known lyrics. They went to the Alpine resort of Thun, where Arnold is thought to have met her, hoping somehow to trace her through the hotel register or through some wispy local tradition of a summer romance between a girl and a dandified young Englishman. The hotel register for that far-away period, however, had been destroyed, and no one in the town remembered having heard his parents or grandparents speak of such a love affair. So they came back to America empty-handed, but with memories of a pleasant outing.

Although I do not have the statistics handy, I imagine that the all-time record for scholarly mileage, at least for mileage expended in the pursuit of a single little cluster of facts, must be held by the man who searched for Sambir. It is a story that deserves to be better known.

Somewhere in Borneo, in 1887–88, there occurred a fortuitous and fateful meeting between a Polish mariner, sailing out of Singapore as first mate of the Arab-owned steamer *Vidar*, and a morose Dutch trader. The sailor was to become famous as Joseph Conrad; the trader was to contribute to the beginnings of Conrad's fame as the inspiration for the protagonist in his first novel, *Almayer's Folly*. Conrad himself always felt that his encounter with "Kaspar Almayer" had been of crucial importance in his career. "If I had not got to know Almayer pretty well," he wrote in *A Personal Record*, "it is almost certain there would never have been a line of mine in print." For, having once met the man, he could not forget him; and even though at that time his literary interests were avowedly those of the amateur – after all, he was a professional seaman, who had just won his master's papers – he got to work on a short novel built about the man he called Almayer. For five years (1889–94) he amused himself with his manuscript, in his leisure hours as second mate aboard a Congo River steamer, later as an unemployed, fever-weakened seaman in Glasgow and London, and finally as first mate of a steamer on the England-Australia run. He had no thought of turning to writing as a career; all his ambition was concentrated upon winning a command of his own. But while he searched for that command his first novel, *Almayer's Folly*, appeared – shortly followed by *An Outcast of the Islands* and *The Nigger of the "Narcissus"* – and Conrad, dogged by ill health and faced with the necessity of supporting a wife and son, reluctantly realized that his future livelihood was not on the bridge but at the writing desk. And so Almayer – whoever he might have been – gave the first impetus to Conrad's career as novelist.

That is one reason why students wanted to know more about the original of Almayer. Another reason is that it has always been known that for his earliest important novels Conrad, like Melville, drew his raw materials directly from his own observations and experiences during his seafaring years. Many of his characters were modeled after men whom he had known in Africa or the Dutch East Indies; many of his basic situations had their real-life counterparts. Therefore, to understand the precise manner in which Conrad's art of fiction developed, it is important to learn, so far as possible, with what sort of raw materials he began, and how he selected and modified them as he worked them into his novels. For instance, was Almayer, in the novel, a fairly faithful representation of the man Conrad had known, and was the story of the novel based on actual events? Or did Conrad merely take certain memorable traits of the man for his portrait of Almayer, and build up about the fictional figure a narrative which had no source in fact?

Conrad, in his autobiographical volume, wrote at some length of the meeting with Almayer (as he also called the real-life figure) in Borneo, but he supplied no clues, geographical or other, which would lead to an identification of the man. In 1924 his biographer, Jean-Aubry, sought out Captain Craig, the master of the *Vidar*, aboard which Conrad had shipped from Singapore to Borneo. Craig, then over seventy, for the first time supplied the historical Almayer with a definite habitation. The village of "Sambir," in Conrad's novel the scene of the struggle between Almayer and the Rajah Lakamba, in reality, said Craig, was the Borneo village of Bulungan forty miles up the Bulungan River; and it was the Bulungan River that Conrad named the "Pantai" – the secret of whose navigable channel only Almayer's father-in-law, Captain Tom Lingard, knew until the day the Arabs discovered it and thus destroyed his trading monopoly.

To Dr. John D. Gordan, now curator of the Berg Collection at The New York Public Library, such a clue was too inviting to be resisted. Twelve years after Jean-Aubry's *Joseph Conrad: Life and Letters* appeared, Gordan, working on his exhaustive study of Conrad's early career as a novelist, decided to follow Conrad to Borneo: indeed, to visit "Sambir" itself, and to find out what he could about the man whom Conrad called Almayer, and about prototypes of the other leading characters in *Almayer's Folly*.

Across the United States he went in the summer of 1939, his wife and sister with him; then by ship to Australia, and finally north by plane to Soerabaja in Java, where he begged the aid of the Bataafsche Petroleum Maatschappij, the great Dutch company some of whose oil fields lay near Bulungan. The officials were polite, helpful, and incredulous. "Obviously," Gordan recalls, "they couldn't imagine what we wanted, and certainly we must have seemed suspicious characters in those days of international competition for oil." But they gave him directions for reaching Bulungan if he really insisted on visiting such a God-forsaken spot in the wilds of Borneo.

Following the directions, Gordan left Soerabaja one Saturday morning by plane, crossing the Java Sea which Conrad had plied in the *Vidar* and halting for passengers at the very ports which he had known. High over Borneo he flew, over the great delta of the Berouw River, at which he gazed with the impersonal interest of the traveler, never dreaming that that area would turn out to have a very direct connection with his search. Then the plane reached the delta of the Bulungan River, in the forested upper reaches of which the village of Bulungan lay hidden, and glided down toward the oil tanks on the island of Tarakan lying offshore.

The Dutch oil officials at Tarakan welcomed Gordan and his companions at the company's *passanggrahan* (rest house); but they also could not conceal their amazement over the purpose of the visit. "We were following the trail of a Polish seaman who had written novels in English about run-to-seed Dutchmen who lived among Malays in Borneo? Obviously we were harmless, and obviously we were crazy." But crazy people must be humored, and so the oil men supplied a motor launch and two native seamen and sent Gordan on his fifty-mile trip across the bay and up the Bulungan River. At last, he exulted, he was on his way to "Sambir"!

The launch sped past the fishing weirs strung like fences in the mouth of the river, and into the maze of channels into which the delta was divided. The palms crowded down to the edge of the water; only occasionally did a native village appear where, as the sun went down, men and children were seen bathing and the smell of wood smoke and cooking food came over the river. It was a strange and not a little unnerving situation for the young Harvard literary scholar: the Malayan seamen could speak no English, and he knew neither Dutch nor Malay; and here he was, in the midst of the tangled Borneo jungle, on his way to a village not even marked on most maps, with the tropical night closing in! But as the stars came out he took comfort in the appearance of the Southern Cross and the Big Dipper; "Sambir" at least was in the same world.

After the launch had pushed up the dark jungle river a few more miles the seamen pointed ahead and began to chatter in their native tongue. There was a glare in the sky – the reflection of the street lights of the Dutch settlement of Bulungan. Arc lights in the remote interior of Borneo! Had Gordan come all these thousands of miles to steep himself in the atmosphere Conrad had known, only to find himself back in twentieth-century western civilization?

But the launch headed for the opposite shore, where the Malay portion of Bulungan, lighted only by feeble oil lamps, straggled along the river. At the landing he was met by Mrs. Fisk, an American missionary to whom the officials of the Bataafsche Petroleum Maatschappij had given him a letter of introduction. Although it was true that her husband was absent in Java assembling a hospital plane with which he planned to extend his mission to the Dyaks still farther inland, she assured Gordan that only in this respect, and that of the arc lights across the river, had Bulungan moved forward since Conrad's time. The arc lights, she explained, had been installed by the reigning sultan, who had become infatuated with such illumination during a visit to the Netherlands – but they were the only modern touch to be found in the vicinity. The next morning he discovered for himself how right she was: "On the Sultan's side of the river was a low line of native houses broken by the cupola of the mosque and the two-story palace, like a small, old-fashioned beach cottage, comfortably surrounded by verandas. Our side of the river also had a two-story building, the combined general store and hotel run by a Chinaman. At the landing stage was a huge banyan tree firmly anchored by its aerial roots, and shading a dark brown godown. The river bank was decorated with crude statues of lions and Malays erected in honor of Queen Wilhelmina by Her Majesty's Dutch, Chinese, and Malay subjects."

So here was Bulungan, a primitive settlement peopled by mixed breeds, almost swallowed up by the Bornean jungle – a settlement right out of the pages of Conrad. Now, what about Almayer and his relatives? In reply to questions, Mrs. Fisk said that although she had lived in the village for many years she could not recall having heard either of Almayer or of his father-in-law, Captain Tom Lingard. However, Lieutenant Boelhouwer of the Dutch garrison might be able to help. So to the lieutenant they went. He too failed to recognize either name, and at this point the quest for Almayer might have ended forever, in a total blank; but in the garrison office was a record clerk, named Pangemanan, who came to the rescue. Yes; he had heard of Captain Tom Lingard. In fact he had himself known Jim, Lingard's swaggering nephew, whom everyone called Tuan (Lord) Jim. Uncle and nephew had traded together until, after a quarrel, the former had returned to England, while Tuan Jim, remaining in Borneo, lived off the profits of money lent to a prominent Chinese merchant. He had died about 1925, leaving several children born to him by his native wife. (In *Almayer's Folly*, too, the elder Lingard had gone back to Europe, after the collapse of his trading monopoly. As for Tuan Jim, in Pangemanan's recollections of him Gordan recognized several characteristics of Conrad's hero in *Lord Jim*.)

Even more exciting, Pangemanan knew who Almayer had been! The name of the man Conrad had met was Olmeijer – he had simply Anglicized the Dutch spelling. Without knowing Conrad's model, Pangemanan had known his family. Olmeijer, he told Gordan, had had several children – not one, as Captain Craig had reported to Jean-Aubry – and one of the daughters had married Andrew Gray of Samarinda, farther down the coast of East Borneo. She was living there now.

The search for Sambir was having its initial fruits. *But* – and here was the shock and surprise of the whole long trip – Bulungan turned out not to be Sambir at all! Pangemanan had known Lingard and the Olmeijers not in Bulungan, but in Berouw – an equally remote settlement on the Berouw River, over which Gordan had flown so carelessly the day before. Because of a slip of Captain Craig's memory in Jean-Aubry's interview with him Gordan had been following the wrong scent all this time; but, by one of those coincidences which sometimes come to the rescue of scholars in their darkest moments, his mistake had turned into good fortune. For in revealing that Bulungan was *not* Sambir, Pangemanan was able to give him fresh clues which he otherwise might never have obtained.

Berouw, the true Sambir, deep in the Bornean jungle, was inaccessible to Gordan; but the fact that one of Olmeijer's daughters was living in Samarinda raised his hopes, for before setting out in the motor launch from Tarakan he had arranged to return to Soerabaja by trading steamer, and the steamer was scheduled to call at Samarinda. Back down the swift Bulungan he went, and thence to the hospitable quarters of the oil men on Tarakan.

The *Van Swoll*, the very sort of steamer upon which Conrad had shipped in these Celebes waters, made a leisurely voyage down the east coast of Borneo. Under a full moon it put into the Kotei River, eventually reaching Samarinda. The captain himself took Gordan to visit Mr. and Mrs. Gray, son-in-law and daughter of Olmeijer. At last, Gordan thought, he was about to meet persons who had actually known the man Conrad knew! But now came a fresh shock. At the family's combination lumber mill, lemonade works, and ice factory, he was told that the Grays no longer lived in Samarinda; they had moved to Malang, in Java. However, their son, who operated these industries, was on his way back from a visit to them, and his ship, the *Pahud*, was to touch at Balikpapan tomorrow, when the *Van Swoll* too would be there.

The next day Gordan, aboard the *Van Swoll*, reached Balikpapan only to find that the *Pahud* had already been in port for several hours and young Mr. Gray had gone off to visit friends in the town; the steward on the *Pahud* did not know who they were. Gordan tried to reach him at the club and the rest house, with no success. Finally, in desperation, he walked the streets looking for a man whom he would not recognize even if he saw him. The *Van Swoll* was getting ready to depart. Gordan dashed back to the *Pahud* – and there Gray was. He records:

> Olmeijer's grandson, short, thick-set, with a clear tan skin and an agreeable smile, said, Yes, he had heard that a certain Conrad had written a story about his grandfather. Had I written it? That was good, because it was not a nice story, it did not tell the truth. He had tried to get the book – wasn't it called "Conrad's Folly"? – sending even to Singapore for it. He confessed that he really knew little about his mother's family. But his parents would certainly see me at Malang to answer all my questions; they too wanted to clear up the falsehoods that this writer had circulated. He would telegraph them that I was coming. We shook hands – I shook hands with a grandson of Almayer's! – and I rushed off to the *Van Swoll*, which was impatiently blasting her whistle.

The round trip from Soerabaja to Tarakan had been a matter of sixteen hundred miles; its net result, in addition, of course, to the collection of a great deal of Conradian local color, was the discovery that Olmeijer's daughter lived in Malang, which was fifty miles from Soerabaja! If Gordan had had the right clue when he set out he could have saved himself a week of travel through Dutch East Borneo. But now, at last, he was on the right track. An hour's train ride took him to the pleasant Javan town of Malang, where the Grays were expecting him. First Mr. Gray, a hearty eighty-year-old Scotsman, had to tell his own story. He had come out to Java in 1879 and, prospering in several businesses, had married Olmeijer's daughter. He had known Captain Craig well, but had never met Conrad.

Then his wife, Johanna Elizabeth, third child in a family of eleven, had her turn. Her father's name, she told Gordan, had been William Charles, not Kaspar (though there was a Kaspar in the family, from whom Conrad had perhaps derived the suggestion). Like Conrad's character, he had left his birthplace in Java for Berouw (Sambir), and he too had been a trader in gutta, rattan, and rubber, highly respected by everyone. In some respects, such as incurring the suspicion of the Dutch authorities because of his friendship with the native Dyaks, and shipping his goods to the outside world through Tom Lingard, Olmeijer's life seems to have directly suggested passages in Conrad's novel. But the more the Grays told of Olmeijer, the clearer it became that in no sense had Conrad used the man as a formal model. Rather, he had taken certain characteristics – his moroseness, his liking for pretentious display, his perpetual sense of frustration – and altered others as he saw fit. It was in this respect, rather than in any attempt to transfer Olmeijer's life literally to his pages, that Conrad may be said to have used the Bornean trader as a model. "Clearly," Gordan says, "*Almayer's Folly* was not a record of the life of William Charles Olmeijer but an expansion of the impression made upon the novelist by the man's personality."

Back in Soerabaja, Gordan had one more call to make
– to the grave of Olmeijer, who had died, according to
Mrs. Gray, not of opium addiction (as the fictional Almayer
did) or of a wound sustained in a python hunt (as Captain
Craig had alleged), but after an operation for cancer. In the
Peneleh Cemetery near the city, a grassless, treeless desert
of whitewashed vaults and graves, Gordan found B821, "a
single low vault like a solid table of whitewashed brick. In
the center of the sloping top was inserted a white marble
plaque almost covered by a wreath of silvered palm leaves."
On the plaque was recorded simply the fact that here lay
Carel Olmeijer, who was born at Grissee (a town north-
west of Soerabaja) in 1799 and died in 1877, "deeply re-
gretted by his children." According to the cemetery records, five of his children were buried in the same vault,
including William Charles. Of the younger Olmeijer's in-
fluence on the life of a great English novelist, no word was
anywhere recorded. Gordan at that moment was the only
man in the world, apart from Olmeijer's family, who knew
that here in Peneleh Cemetery was the grave of the man
who had inspired Conrad to become a novelist. But the discovery had been worth a trip halfway around the world.

Essays by John D. Gordan

A Doctor's Benefaction

The Berg Collection
at The New York Public Library

◆

NEW YORK CITY has been unusually fortunate in the number of rare books and important manuscripts which generous citizens have given to the public. Few institutions have been more handsomely treated over the years than The New York Public Library. Since the library of James Lenox became part of the original incorporation, the Library has received no gifts of books and manuscripts richer than those of Dr. Albert Ashton Berg. It was during Harry Miller Lydenberg's time as Director that Dr. Berg made his three great benefactions. If it had not been for H.M.L., for his enthusiasm and for his diplomacy, the Library might not today house the Henry W. and Albert A. Berg Collection in Memory of Henry W. Berg.

Though the Collection reflects the interests of two medical men, it was not medical material that attracted Dr. Henry W. and Dr. A. A. Berg. Their interest was in English and American literature. During his lifetime Dr. A. A. gave approximately forty thousand items to the Library. Half of these, roughly, were printed material, and half manuscript. The printed items, be they broadside, pamphlet in soft covers, or book in hard, are generally first editions. Occasionally there will be a later printing with significant changes of text. Among the printed material should be included various kinds of proof sheets; much of this proof is corrected in longhand. There are no manuscripts of the period before printing. The manuscript material comprises authors' manuscripts and letters, as well as authors' typescripts, generally corrected by hand, and typewritten letters.

The Berg Collection is essentially an author collection. It is not a collection devoted to a subject, like drama or poetry or the novel, or to a type, like incunabula or broadsides. It has been built up by collectors who were interested in the great figures of English and American literature and in many of lesser rank. These collectors gathered together as much printed and manuscript material by each writer as opportunity, their interest, and their pocketbooks allowed – and there have been some deep pocketbooks connected with the formation of the Berg Collection.

The formation of the Collection makes a dramatic story. In the first fifteen months of its life as part of The New York Public Library, it grew from about three thousand to some thirty thousand items. This was an increase not only in quantity, but in quality. No such staggering rate of growth could have been achieved without massive additions, and the Berg Collection grew, as have almost all the great libraries of the world, by the acquisition of other entire collections as well as of single pieces. Dr. Berg added two famous collections to his original gift of his own. We at the Library have a keen interest in the development of these two collections when they were in private hands, and in the collectors whose tastes shaped this development. Our chief interest is, naturally, in Dr. Berg, as the benefactor responsible for the final deposit at Fifth Avenue and Forty-Second Street of all this material.

The first gift which Dr. A. A. made to the Library was the three thousand or so items which he and his brother Dr. Henry W. had assembled over three decades. The brothers had been wide readers in English and American literature. As boys they had worked in the library of Cooper Union, where they had plenty of time for browsing. There was a family tradition that Henry had recited the closing lines of "Thanatopsis" to Bryant when the poet visited the institute one day. Another tradition was that Albert had developed a taste for Dickens at the age of five or six. Ultimately this fondness led him into collecting first editions, as distinguished from a reading library. In all likelihood it was their early reading which turned two doctors – the elder a specialist in the treatment of smallpox and diphtheria, the younger a world authority on the treatment of cancer and ulcers of the stomach and of cancer of the gastrointestinal tract – away from a "shop collection" of medical books to a collection of literary material.

Dr. A. A. began the collecting. His first purchase of a rare book was of a Dickens novel in parts; just which novel, unhappily, he could never remember. This was around 1910, and since the brothers shared their interests, Dr. Henry W. was soon an enthusiast. As a curb on their enthusiasm, they set themselves a limit of $100 an item. The curb did not hold for long, or the collection which they had built up by the time of Doctor Henry W.'s death in December 1938 would not have been so good as it was.

A year or so before the elder Doctor's death, the brothers approached The New York Public Library to discuss presenting their collection to the Library. They stipulated that they wanted a separate room for their books and would provide a fund for its upkeep. This generous offer put the Board of Trustees in a quandary, because space is almost the most precious thing in a great library today. The Board's acceptance of the Berg Collection turned out, however, to be one of its wisest decisions. It took some time to work out details to the satisfaction of the Doctors, and before final arrangements were made Dr. Henry W. died. Dr. A. A. desired to carry through the gift as a memorial to his brother. In 1939 the remaining details were settled, and on February 6, 1940, the Doctor made a formal offer which the Trustees accepted on February 14.

Once the memorial to Dr. Henry W. had been established and their private collection turned over to the public, Dr. A. A. found his desire to build up the Collection strengthened. Quite possibly, since he would now be buying material for an institution instead of for his own library, his dislike of self-indulgence was no longer a deterrent to large expenditure. His native shrewdness, furthermore, prompted him to take advantage of opportunities to purchase two great collections *en bloc*. Though the amounts paid were too large for the purchases to be classed as bargains, they were small in comparison with the sums that had been put into building up these same collections in a time of mounting prices.

The first opportunity came after the death of William Thomas Hildrup Howe of Cincinnati. A New Englander by birth and a graduate of Yale, Mr. Howe had been for many years President of the American Book Company. He, too, was a bachelor, and for some forty years he had pursued the hobby of collecting – old American glass as well as books and manuscripts – with even more ardor than the Doctors. His interest was also in English and American literature, particularly of the nineteenth and early twentieth centuries. Some of the authors whom he collected, like John Galsworthy and James Stephens, had been his friends, had visited him, and had written to him frequently. Most of Howe's library was in Kentucky, at "Freelands," the house which he named after Galsworthy's novel and which appears on his bookplate. In its particular field the Howe collection was known to be one of the richest in private hands, and after Mr. Howe died intestate in August 1939, several institutions began angling for it.

Dr. Berg's attention was first directed to the collection in August 1940 by one of the most interesting personalities in the rare book world, the late Mitchell Kennerley. As his success with the Anderson Galleries indicated, Kennerley was a showman of charm and persuasion. He was acting for a well-known Chicago dealer, Walter M. Hill, who represented the Howe estate. The man who really heated to incandescence Dr. Berg's desire to have the Howe collection was Robert M. Lingel, then Chief of the Library's Acquisition Division. Lingel was a master salesman, and he knew how to reconcile interests that were apparently in hopeless conflict: the seller, the buyer, the agent – even two agents! Kennerley and Lingel are both now dead, and it is genuinely distressing to remember that their latter days were not happy. The Berg Collection would not be the outstanding collection that it is today had it not been for these two men.

Negotiations were carried on, at whirlwind speed for such a sizable transaction, during late August and early September 1940. Lingel and Kennerley made a flying trip to Chicago and Cincinnati; Lingel flew back to Cincinnati for a few hours to obtain an option; and on September 12 the sale was clinched in Philadelphia, where the attorney for the estate happened to be at the moment. The sixteen thousand or so books and manuscripts which made up the Howe collection arrived at The New York Public Library on September 24 to be checked off by Library officials, by Miss Edith Tranter (the executor of Mr. Howe's estate), by Walter Hill, and by Mitchell Kennerley. On November 13, the Howe library became officially a part of the Berg Collection.

A few months later, Kennerley came to Dr. Berg with another project. Mr. Owen D. Young, the retired head of the General Electric Company, was anxious to dispose of the collection of more than ten thousand English and American literary first editions and manuscripts which he had been building up for thirty years. This hobby Mr. Young had been able to pursue despite the fact that, unlike the other collectors about whom we have been talking, he was not a bachelor. Born in Van Hornesville, New York, in 1874, the same year as W. T. H. Howe, he has been twice married. It is a pleasure to be able to say that – again unlike so many of the other figures in this story – he is still hale and hearty. It was in order to provide for benefactions of his own in the neighborhood of Van Hornesville that he decided to sell his library. Apparently he had thought of offering several institutions an opportunity to make purchases and had even placed some items with a well-known rare book firm in New York. He had retained Mitchell Kennerley as appraiser and, presumably, as agent.

Once again it was Robert Lingel who fired Dr. Berg with the desire to add the Young collection to his other gifts to the Library. The situation also called for the miraculous ability of the Chief of the Acquisition Division to reconcile apparent irreconcilables. By refusing to take "No" for an answer, by traveling back and forth between New York and Florida, Lingel brought about an acceptable arrangement. Dr. Berg purchased an undivided half-interest in the Young collection for the Library, and Mr. Young presented the remainder. The whole was to become a part of the Berg Collection. This magnificent joint gift was announced on the front pages of the New York papers on May 5, 1941. Thus the tenfold growth of the Berg Collection came about within fifteen months of the Doctor's original gift.

By the spring of 1941, the Berg Collection had reached the same general proportions that it will have for many years to come, even though it steadily increases in size. In range, it extends from the end of the fifteenth century to the early twentieth. Practically, this means that it has a handful of English incunables, and that the most recent of its authors had attained some reputation by the time of the First World War. The strength of the Collection varies greatly over the range of four or more centuries. It is hardly surprising that it contains no material of the Anglo-Saxon period. It is scarcely more surprising that there is no medieval material, except two chronicles printed by Caxton and one by Wynkyn de Worde. There is little of the early Renaissance, but that little is choice. It has, among other first printings, a perfect copy of John Foxe's *Actes and Monuments*, or *Book of Martyrs*; the sixth edition of *Songes and Sonnets*, better known as *Tottel's Miscellany*; a perfect copy of the first English comedy, *Gammer Gurton's Needle*; two titles by John Shelton; and two by John Heywood.

It is only with the late Elizabethan period that the Collection begins to achieve any wide coverage, any density. Over the next two hundred years of English literature it gradually increases in strength until by the eighteenth century it can be said to have excellent but not exhaustive runs of books by the important authors. For the period up to 1641 covered by *A Short-Title Catalogue*, there are in the Berg Collection only 319 titles, some of which are present in more than one copy. It should be borne in mind that these are works of literature, not the religious or governmental publications that so enormously swell the number of entries in STC. There are, for instance, half a dozen Edmund Spensers, including several variants of *The Faerie Queene*, two copies of *Colin Clout*, and two of the *Complaints*, as well as *Fowre Hymnes* and *Prothalamion*. Sidney is represented by *An Apologie for Poetrie* and *The Countesse of Pembrokes Arcadia*, perfect except for a missing blank leaf. There are half a dozen Ben Jonson firsts in addition to the *Workes*, and a dozen and a half of George Chapman's with all his translations of Homer. Other Stuart dramatists – Beaumont and Fletcher, Dekker, John Ford, Heywood, Middleton, Shirley, Webster – are well represented. The collection, however, has only one manuscript of the period before 1641, but an important one: John Donne's poems dating from 1619, formerly in the possession of the Earls of Westmorland.

No attempt has yet been made to check off Berg holdings in Donald Wing's helpful extension of the Pollard and Redgrave *Short-Title Catalogue*. The Collection has reasonably good resources for the major figure of the mid-century, John Milton – twenty-seven titles, including "Lycidas," "Comus," and all six title-pages of the first printings of *Paradise Lost*. The Cavalier poets, the metaphysical poets, the great prose writers like Browne and Burton and Walton, are well accounted for, the first four editions of *The Compleat Angler* being present. Dryden, the great figure of the latter half of the seventeenth century, is represented by thirty-five titles. There is only a weak collection of late seventeenth-century dramatists, though there are four original letters of William Congreve's, whose letters are notably scarce. There are few other autograph letters by seventeenth-century figures.

The strength of the Berg Collection is greater in the eighteenth than in the seventeenth century, and it waxes with the century. There are fair to good collections of the important figures of the earlier half – Defoe, Swift, Addison, Steele, Edward Young, Gay, Pope, Richardson, Fielding, William Collins, Thomas Gray; and of the latter half – Dr. Johnson, Sterne, Smollett, Goldsmith, Cowper, Sheridan, Crabbe, Burns, Blake, Jane Austen, and lesser figures. In the eighteenth century the Collection increases in interest for the manuscript material and autograph letters it contains. Of the twenty-one writers just mentioned, all but three

(Collins, Fielding, and Gay) are at least represented by autograph letters, and all but Addison, Defoe, Blake, and Young
by manuscript material as well as by letters. The most important of the manuscript material is a rough draft of the
first three books of Pope's *Essay on Man*. Two of the collections of letters are sizable; there are fifty by Thomas Gray,
and fifty-three by Dr. Johnson. These holdings, however,
are small indeed by comparison with the Burney papers
belonging to the latter half of the century. In the Collection
are the manuscripts of Fanny Burney's *Evelina*, *Cecilia*, *Ca-
milla*, and of her *Diary and Letters* as prepared for the press.
There are manuscripts of seventeen additional diaries, nine
unpublished plays, and twenty notebooks. In addition, Berg
has nine hundred autograph letters of Fanny Burney's as
well as several hundred of other members of the Burney
family.

It must be remembered that the material in the Berg
Collection from 1500 to 1800 has come almost entirely from
the joining together of what Mr. Young and the Doctors
had collected, and that these collectors had large nineteenth-
century holdings as well. Considerably less than half the
thirty thousand items of the combined Berg, Howe, and
Young collections are reflected in these three centuries. It is
not surprising, therefore, to find that its nineteenth-century
material, English and American, is Berg's strength and its
treasure. The collections of books by the principal authors
of the century are gratifyingly close to completion, even
including two of such rarities as the Bristol edition of Wordsworth and Coleridge's *Lyrical Ballads*, Browning's *Pauline*,

Bryant's *Embargo*, and Poe's *Tamerlane*, to mention only the more spectacular.

It is the manuscript material that makes the Collection particularly interesting to scholars of this period. It is tempting to adduce a host of examples, but a half dozen or so must represent the rest. Take, for instance, the Coleridge material: there are thirty manuscripts, three notebooks, and over one hundred autograph letters. There are some three hundred Thackeray autograph letters and five hundred Dickens autograph letters, as well as minor manuscripts by both men. The turn of the century is well exemplified by Kipling, of whom we have two dozen manuscripts (including a manuscript of *Departmental Ditties*), 125 drawings, and over one hundred letters. In American literature Berg contains interesting Hawthorne material: some dozen minor manuscripts, an Italian diary and notebook, and 220 letters. This is backed up by a massive collection of a dozen or so diaries and several hundred letters of Sophia Hawthorne's and her sisters'. There are better than 1,700 pages of Thoreau's nature studies, and fifty of his letters. Whitman is represented by twenty manuscripts and 385 autograph letters. Clemens, at the turn of the century, can be studied in fifty manuscripts, including *A Connecticut Yankee*, *Following the Equator*, and *Tom Sawyer Abroad*, and four hundred autograph letters.

The Berg Collection is unusually rich in association volumes among its nineteenth-century holdings. There are, for instance, five presentation copies of *A Week on the Concord and Merrimack Rivers* – those given by Thoreau to William Cullen Bryant, Ellery Channing, Ralph Waldo Emerson, James Anthony Froude, and Nathaniel Hawthorne. On the more sentimental side, Berg has some fascinating dedication copies. It has, for example, the copy of *The Raven and Other Poems* (New York, 1845) sent by Poe to Elizabeth Barrett, later Mrs. Robert Browning, and the letter she wrote thanking Poe for the dedication and the book. It has the copy of *Vanity Fair* given by Thackeray to Bryan Waller Procter, who wrote poetry under the name of Barry Cornwall, and the copy of *The History of Pendennis* given Dr. John Elliotson, the physician who pulled Thackeray through a desperate illness. For sentimental interest few books can surpass the copy of *Alice's Adventures in Wonderland* which Dodgson gave Alice Pleasance Liddell, or the copy of *A Child's Garden of Verses* which Stevenson sent Alison Cunningham. Both are in the Berg Collection.

There is one aspect of the Collection which makes it of unusual usefulness, especially to bibliographers. It so often contains two or more copies of the first edition of a title. This situation has come about from the merging of three private libraries. It has already been pointed out that even in the period prior to 1800, where repetition would occur only between the smaller Berg and Young libraries, there is often more than one copy of a book. In the nineteenth century, when the Howe library, larger than both the others put together, enters the picture, the duplication of titles becomes heavy. Mr. Howe, furthermore, understood the value of comparing copies of a title, and he often deliberately bought more than one copy.

The value of such multiplicity to the scholar, of course, lies in the variants, states, and issues of the text and binding of a first edition which can be brought to light by comparison. Berg has, for example, four copies of the Aylott and Jones, 1846, edition of the Brontës' *Poems*, and among these are three variant bindings. In the investigations carried on by Mr. Jacob Blanck for the forthcoming *Bibliography of American Literature*, under the auspices of this Society, it was a considerable advantage to find in the Berg Collection, for instance, nine copies of *The Scarlet Letter* and eleven copies of *The House of the Seven Gables*. When a careful bibliography on Dickens is made, it will be useful to have in the Collection seven copies of *The Posthumous Papers of the Pickwick Club* in parts.

In closing, I should like to say something about the probable future growth of the Collection. The direction of this growth was taken, with the Doctor's approval, in the dozen years between the gift of Mr. Young's library and the present, during which roughly ten thousand items have been added. Emphasis has been laid upon the acquisition of manuscript material, because scholars have shown themselves on the whole more interested in the written than in the printed word. Income for new acquisitions is not yet available from the munificent legacy the Doctor left the Collection, because of plans for a new stack. When the Collection has this income to spend, the acquisition of manuscripts will doubtless still be the primary interest. Close to that aim will be the completing, insofar as possible, of the runs of printed material and the strengthening of the periods in which this review has shown the Collection to be weak. The Collection has always been considered part of The New York Public Library and not a separate entity in itself, and consequently the building-up of its printed sources will not, except for a special purpose, duplicate what is elsewhere in the Library. In his own lifetime, Dr. Berg carried his benefaction to eminence, and by his princely bequest he made it possible for the growth and usefulness of the Collection to continue. All of us at the Library will do our best to see that his wishes are carried out.

Charles Dickens

An Exhibition of Manuscripts, Autograph Letters,
and First Editions

◆

THE FIRST EXHIBITION OF MATERIAL from the Henry W. and Albert A. Berg Collection was opened to the public on December 16, 1941, in the Lenox Gallery, which Dr. Albert A. Berg has recently had redecorated as one of his munificent gifts to the Library. The walls have been paneled in oak to harmonize with the adjoining Berg Memorial Room and the lighting fixtures have been modernized so as to present to the best advantage the collection of pictures by Gainsborough, Reynolds, Gilbert Stuart, Turner, and other masters which were in the Lenox bequest. Part of the Berg Collection of rare books and manuscripts, not yet ready for the use of students and scholars, will be housed in low shelves occupying the floor of the room. On top of the bookshelves special cases have been placed to provide for frequent exhibitions of material from the Collection.

The first exhibition is devoted exclusively to the work of Charles Dickens. On display are original manuscripts, autograph letters, and first editions, both in parts and in book form. Many of the copies were presentations from the author to his friends. There is a group of the readings which were prepared by Dickens himself for his four tours. Original drawings for some of the illustrations in the novels, material relating to Dickens' interest in the theatre, and other items connected with his literary and private life are also on view.

Interest in Dickens is perennial, and at no season of the year more than at Christmas, a festival with which many of his stories are intimately associated.

During 1941 several important and delightful studies of his career have been added to the wealth of critical and biographical material already in print, yet it is not his literary importance alone that motivates this exhibition. Gratitude plays a leading part. It is largely to Charles Dickens that the Library owes the gifts which it has received from Dr. Albert Berg. His boyhood fondness for Dickens developed into a general love of books. This in turn produced a desire to collect. And the first purchase of the collector was one of his favorite's novels in parts.

All the material exhibited here has been drawn from the Berg Collection. This singleness of source is noteworthy. There have been in the past magnificent Dickens loan exhibitions, built up from many sources. The New York Public Library is fortunate in having an unusually rich store of Dickens material in one collection. This it owes to the imagination and diligence of Dr. Berg, the late W. T. H. Howe, and Mr. Owen D. Young, whose libraries have been merged in the Berg Collection.

The material has been arranged for the sake of simplicity by subject and by chronology. In the outer row of cases, beginning on the left of the door from the corridor, are shown Dickens' novels and sketches as he produced them year by year. The history of each production has been traced in detail. Whenever it was possible, a page of the original manuscript has been exhibited to display his methods of composition and the earliest state of a story. Autograph letters are shown in connection with the development of a story and of Dickens' career. Publication has been followed through successive stages – the appearance in monthly parts, in book form, and in reprint, including the American pirated and authorized editions. In addition many imitations and continuations of the novels by other hands testify to Dickens' popularity. The novelist's activities as editor and journalist are briefly represented.

The cases in the outer row on the south of the room contain the Christmas books and the Christmas numbers of Dickens' periodicals, which have been grouped together for convenience. The Christmas stories were enthusiastically received on both sides of the Atlantic, and the characters in *A Christmas Carol* are almost as well known as Santa Claus.

Following the Christmas productions comes a display relating to Dickens' public readings from his own work. This secondary career, a natural outgrowth of his life-long interest in the theatre, earned him a small fortune and hastened his early death. The strain of the readings is clear from the schedules for the four tours. A unique exhibit is the group of reading copies prepared by him for his own use on the platform.

Another display in the outer row of cases comprises a run of the *Gad's Hill Gazette*. This amateur newspaper was put out by Dickens' son, Henry Fielding Dickens, with the aid of the entire family circle, including the novelist. Last of all, the figurines in Doulton and other porcelain demonstrate what a place Dickens' characters have taken among the lasting creations of the imagination.

In the cases in the center of the room, opposite the door to the corridor, there are arranged in chronological order numerous original drawings for the illustrations of many of Dickens' stories. The artists worked in pencil, ink, wash, and watercolor. Most of the drawings are, naturally, by Hablot Knight Browne, better known as Phiz, who illustrated so many of the works of Dickens. In later years he made copies of his illustrations for several of the novels – *Bleak House, Dombey and Son, Little Dorrit,* and *Martin Chuzzlewit* – as special commissions for an admirer. The albums are on display here, though unfortunately only one sketch from each can be shown. There are other drawings by artists who tried their hand at "extra-illustrations," sometime after the original publications had appeared. Altogether they show the happy collaboration of the talents of novelist and artist.

Next in order will be found material relating to Dickens' interest in the theatre, which was strong from his boyhood. An ardent theatregoer, he was also an unusually talented amateur actor and producer. There are displayed numerous programs of plays in which he acted and plays which he directed. Each of his own plays and of his collaborations with Wilkie Collins is exhibited, in some cases in manuscript as well as published form. Of course, there were innumerable dramatizations of his stories by other pens, and these attempts, which generally caused Dickens acute embarrassment, are well represented.

Finally copies are exhibited of most of his important books bearing inscriptions in his own hand. The relationships which they reveal are representative of a man who made friends readily. Here are presentations to members of his immediate family circle and to more distant relatives of his own and his wife's. Among his friends, the man of affairs, the doctor, the clergyman, the lawyer, the scholar, the writer, and the artist are all to be found. Furthermore the range is international, including Great Britain, the Continent, and the United States.

The explanatory cards try to give a few pertinent facts about each item and to present a brief account of Dickens' literary activities. For the most part, the information given does not deal with bibliographical detail; the collector will recognize the rarities without trouble. Indeed, the material will speak for itself to all comers, to the bibliophile, to the student, and to those who want only to renew old friendships with stories and characters they have loved since childhood.

The Secret of
Dickens' Memoranda

◆

ON NOVEMBER 9, 1867, Charles Dickens sailed on the *Cuba* from Liverpool for Boston on his second American tour. Though increasing ill-health made the enterprise unwise, his emotional instability of the past decade and an increasing desire for money, whetted by the profits to be derived from public readings, drove him on. He put his affairs in order for the journey. In the week before he left[1] he made out a list with eight entries, headed Memoranda, for William Henry Wills, his assistant editor on *All the Year Round* and his good friend and adviser. The Memoranda were apparently first published in R. C. Lehmann's *Charles Dickens as Editor; Being Letters Written by Him to William Henry Wills His Subeditor* (New York, 1912), p. 365–367, and reprinted by Walter Dexter in the Nonesuch edition of the collected *Letters*, III, 563.[2] The original manuscript is now in the Henry W. and Albert A. Berg Collection in The New York Public Library, but cannot be reproduced because of copyright.

In the printed text no hint is given of the most arresting thing about the Memoranda: the mysterious blotting out of the fifth memorandum. Dickens wrote with his characteristic blue ink, and the deletion was made with black ink and thoroughly, except for seven nonconsecutive words missed by the pen. The obliteration, it is believed, was the work of his eldest daughter, Mamie Dickens, or his sister-in-law, Georgina Hogarth. All letters to Wills were apparently lent to them when they were preparing the first collected edition of the novelist's letters, published in 1880–82. Though they did not print the Memoranda, they would have had the opportunity to delete any passage they thought inconsistent with the Dickens legend. Lehmann, Wills's greatnephew, who inherited the correspondence, respected the wishes of the family in his publication of it. He was even careful to omit a clause in the seventh memorandum which had escaped Miss Hogarth's censorial eye and which was a clue to the offending passage.

Before we pry into the secret with infrared photography, let us consider briefly the innocuous memoranda which have long been in print. The first memorandum was concerned with a few last-minute instructions about *All the Year Round*. No allusions were to be made except by Dickens himself to the United States or to the Fenians, the Irish-American political brotherhood founded in 1858 and directed against Great Britain. Either topic, injudiciously handled, might have wrecked the reading tour. Wills was reminded of two imminent contributions: a poem by Mrs. Charles Cowden Clarke, the sentimentally psychic narrative called "The Yule Log," which appeared in the issue of December 21, 1867, and an article by Sir James Emerson Tennent, "The Killing of Dr. Parkman," which appeared in the issue of December 14.[3] In 1849 John W. Webster, Professor of Chemistry at Harvard, had killed Dr. George

Parkman, to whom he owed money, and had tried to dispose of the body in his laboratory. Dickens was fascinated by the murder, for he had met the murderer on his first visit to Boston in 1842. And in December 1867 he could not resist visiting the scene of the crime.

Six of the memoranda dealt with business affairs and financial obligations to dependents. Wills was to attend to all letters, and John Forster, who had Dickens' power of attorney, was to help with matters involving legal opinion. An allowance of one pound each a week was to be paid every Saturday to Mrs. Scott, Mrs. Kelly, and Mrs. Allison, wives of the men whom he took to the United States in his entourage: Scott was his dresser, and Allison the stage gasman. Dickens also made arrangements for an allowance for John Poole, an impoverished dramatist, approximately eighty-one years old, whom he had been helping since 1847.[4] He even gave Wills instructions for the old man's funeral, but Poole outlived his benefactor by two years.

Dickens did not forget the dependents in his own family. Miss Hogarth and Mamie Dickens were given authority to draw checks on his account at Coutts's Bank. He left particular instructions as to his youngest and favorite son, Plorn, Edward Bulwer Lytton Dickens, then nearly sixteen years old. The boy was restless and not studious, and his father had decided that he should make a career for himself in Australia. He wanted Plorn to live with a sheep farmer in preparation for his new life in the colonies. Wills was to find the right farmer, with the help of Samuel Sidney, a contributor to *All the Year Round*, editor of *Sidney's Emigrant's Journal* in 1848–50, and secretary of the Agricultural

Hall Company since 1860. Apparently Wills decided that the Agricultural College, Cirencester, was the solution for Plorn. Though the boy went out to Australia in September 1868 as a sheep farmer, he did not like or succeed in the life.[5]

The secret of the Memoranda does not lie in any of the matters already discussed, though a clue to the blotting can be found in a passage that escaped the obliterating pen of Georgina Hogarth. In the memorandum dealing with John Forster's power of attorney Dickens had added, obviously as an afterthought, that Forster knew about Nelly and would cooperate with Wills in any matter concerning her. The tell-tale reference was omitted when the Memoranda were printed. Like many open secrets, Dickens' love for Ellen Lawless Ternan was discreetly handled for two generations. His contemporaries generally avoided the dangerous subject of his separation from Mrs. Dickens. Edmund Yates made it clear that he was silenced by loyalty. Thomas Adolphus Trollope was emphatic in hoping that his recollection would offend no one and in announcing that he had Miss Hogarth's permission to quote from Dickens' letters. John Bigelow, however, declared with blunt inexactitude that the trouble between the Dickenses was over a Miss Teman, the novelist's mistress.[6] The details were first given to the public by Thomas Wright, who held back the story for thirty years, in an article in the *Daily Express* on April 3, 1934, followed two years later by his *Life of Charles Dickens*. In 1939 in *Dickens and Daughter*, Gladys Storey gave further information which she had received from Kate Dickens Perugini.

Ellen Lawless Ternan came of a family of actors. Her mother was an actress, Frances Eleanor Jarman, and her father was an actor-manager, Thomas Lawless Ternan, who, according to Macready, died in a lunatic asylum in 1846. Ellen and her two sisters, Frances Eleanor and Maria, were trained for the stage. They seem to have been members of the Charles Kean Company at the Royal Princess's Theatre, Oxford Street, when Dickens met them. Mrs. Ternan, Ellen, and Maria were engaged to act in *The Frozen Deep*, by Wilkie Collins, in which Dickens took the leading part, when it was played in Manchester in August 1857 as part of the Douglas Jerrold benefit. Dickens is supposed to have realized he was in love with Ellen on the evening of the last performance. She was eighteen, blonde, petite, and pretty. Presumably she did not become his mistress until after he and Mrs. Dickens had separated in May 1858. He took a house for her at 2 Houghton Place, Ampthill Square, the address given for her in his will. She bore him a son who died in infancy. The relationship was not happy: Dickens seems to have been in love with her youth, and she with his fame and wealth. He was aware that a feeling of guilt haunted her. In an ambiguous letter of July 1867, he admitted that it would cost Nelly her "pride and self-reliance" if she thought her true relations with him were known.[7] Yet she seems to have been on good terms with the members of the family at Gad's Hill. She was summoned at the time of the novelist's death and she remained a friend of Miss Hogarth and Kate Dickens Perugini. The memory of her affair with Dickens seems to have filled her with disgust and remorse. Later she married George Wharton Robinson, a schoolmaster or clergyman, possibly both, and bore him children.[8]

An infrared photograph of the blotted memorandum brings to light what Nelly did while the novelist was on his American tour. It also prompts research into hitherto neglected facts about her life with her family. The passage expunged by Miss Hogarth contained the actress's address: the Villa Trollope, Ricorboli, Florence. Dickens wrote it out twice in case Wills should find it difficult to read. Ellen was to appeal to Wills if she needed any help and to let him know if she moved.

The Villa Trollope was the home of Thomas Adolphus Trollope and his second wife, Frances Eleanor Ternan, Nelly's sister, who were known as the Italian Trollopes. Trollope had settled in Florence almost a quarter of a century before and there had married first Theodosia Garrow, an exotic creature half Jewish, a quarter Scotch, and a quarter Brahmin. Seventeen years later, in April 1865, she died leaving him with an adolescent daughter to care for. He sold the elaborate house in which they had lived and bought a small villa at Ricorboli, a suburb, on the left bank of the Arno below San Miniato al Monte. In the spring of 1866 he asked Frances Ternan to come out from England to look after his daughter. Trollope and his first wife had known and liked Miss Ternan when she had been in Florence studying music under Romani. The situation developed conventionally. Before the end of the summer of 1866 Trollope and Miss Ternan were engaged; they were married in

Paris on October 29; and in July 1867 the daughter was sent off for a year in England.[9]

It is difficult to tell just how friendly was the relationship between Mr. and Mrs. Trollope and Dickens and Ellen Ternan. In a sense Dickens was responsible for Trollope's second marriage. When Frances Ternan went to Florence to study music, he had given her on September 20, 1858, a most friendly letter to Trollope's mother, the well-known novelist, who introduced the girl to her son.[10] Trollope and Dickens had been good friends since 1845, and Frances and Ellen were sisters. Not only were the Italian Trollopes frequent contributors to *All the Year Round*, but Dickens went out of his way to praise Mrs. Trollope's stories, especially *Aunt Margaret's Trouble*. Yet when he congratulated Trollope on his marriage he wrote belatedly and guardedly. And in July 1867, in a letter to a friend who knew the truth about Ellen, he declared that he did not like Frances Ternan Trollope personally and only put up with her because she was Ellen's sister. Furthermore he warned the friend not to mention him around the Trollopes. The implication is that he did not think they knew of his affair with Nelly. Certainly it must have been difficult, if not impossible, to keep the secret from the rest of the Ternans since Ellen and her mother had been living in a house provided by Dickens. And could Nelly have continued to conceal the affair when she visited the Trollopes during Dickens' absence in the United States?[11]

The blotted memorandum suggests that Ellen had gone to Florence before Dickens sailed for Boston in November

1867. She was certainly there in January 1868. In his autobiography Trollope recalled that on January 13, he, his
wife, and her sister, who was staying with them, set out for
Naples to see Vesuvius in eruption. They had a picturesque
time. On a cold, moonless night they went up the moun-
tain, the ladies on ponies, in a great crowd of sightseers carrying torches and following the stream of burning lava.
Later they stayed at Salerno and visited the ruins at Paestum,
then a district infested with banditti. Trollope did not say
how much of the winter Ellen stayed with them, though he
described the gaiety of the carnival that year and trips to the
theatre to see Salvini, the cold and the open fires at the villa.
Perhaps she remained in Florence until Dickens returned to
England in May. Her relationship with the Trollopes must
have been close. After Dickens' death in June 1870 – an
event of which Trollope made no mention – she seems to
have taken refuge with them once more. She went to them
despite the chaos in which the Franco-Prussian War had
thrown the Continent, despite a trying sea voyage and fifteen days in quarantine at Genoa.[12]

There is another detail that emerges from beneath Miss
Hogarth's blottings. Dickens told Wills that he would cable
on his arrival in Boston and asked him to relay the message
to Gad's Hill and to Forster. He also asked him to send the
message verbatim to Ellen in Florence, for the words would
have a special meaning for her. The cable was printed by
Lehmann and by Dexter and was innocuous enough: "Safe
and well expect letter full of hope."[13] What the message
meant to Nelly will probably never be known. Yet even
the surface meaning stirs the imagination when one thinks

of the ill and aging lover and remorseful young woman who was his mistress.

Surely there was nothing in the memorandum itself that induced Miss Hogarth to dip her pen in the blackest ink. It was simply a clue to an unflattering, a tragic episode in the life of her hero. What was her feeling as she blotted out the words? Vigilance for the reputation of the novelist? Care for the good name of the Dickens family? Jealousy of Ellen or a desire to protect her? The instructions restored by the camera are of no great moment in the story of Charles Dickens and Ellen Ternan. But the information given adds its mite to our knowledge of an episode in the life of a genius who was also an unhappy man.

Notes

[1] In *The Letters of Charles Dickens* (The Nonesuch Dickens; Blooms-bury, 1938, III, 563), Walter Dexter, the editor, dated the document "(October 1867)." Yet it must have been written between Saturday, November 2, and Saturday, November 9, for Dickens referred to "this next Saturday, the day of my leaving Liverpool."

[2] Though Dexter did not give his source for the Memoranda, he seems to have copied them from Lehmann, for he gave the same text, even making the same omissions, and used Lehmann's punctuation. The text and punctuation both differ from the original.

[3] These two articles were identified by R. C. Lehmann, who incorrectly dated them December 27 and December 7; Dexter copied the mistaken dates. Dickens had accepted Mrs. Clarke's poem on June 17, 1867 (Charles and Mary Cowden Clarke, *Recollections of Writers* [London, 1878], p. 339; the letter was reprinted by Dexter in the Nonesuch *Letters*, III, 532–533).

[4] John Forster, *The Life of Charles Dickens* (Philadelphia, 1872–74), II, 369–370, 393. The accountants' report for the Hunt-Poole theatrical benefits, dated August 25, 1847, which is now in the Berg Collection, indicates that not enough money was raised to allow anything for Poole.

[5] Nonesuch *Letters*, III, 595, 668, and Gladys Storey, *Dickens and Daughter* (London, [1939]), p. 124, 128, 132, 154, 169–176.

[6] *Edmund Yates: His Recollections and Experiences* (London, 1884), II, 98; Thomas Adolphus Trollope, *What I Remember* (New York, 1888–90), [I], 521–522, 358, note; and John Bigelow, *Retrospections of an Active Life* (New York, 1909–13), I, 264, and IV, 383. Bigelow's Teman is an obvious misreading for Ternan; he also gave Mrs. Ternan's maiden name as Jarmain instead of Jarman.

[7] Nonesuch *Letters*, III, 475–476. The dating of this letter, which was in the collection of the Comte de Suzannet, presents a problem. The date given in the Nonesuch *Letters* is "Thursday Fifth July, 1866."

When the letter was sold at Sotheby's on July 11, 1938 (item 139), it was dated "4 July 1866 [for 1867]." References in the letter to Dolby's trip to the United States to prepare for Dickens' visit definitely place the year as 1867. The correct date, therefore, seems to be Thursday, July 4, 1867.

8 Thomas Wright, *The Life of Charles Dickens* (New York, 1936), p. 241–243, 252–257, 264–268, 280, 356; William Toynbee, ed., *The Diaries of William Macready* (London, 1912), II, 347; Charles Churchill Osborne, ed., *The Letters of Charles Dickens to the Baroness Burdett-Coutts* (New York, [1932]), p. 185–186; Storey, *Dickens*, p. 90, 93, 94, 137.

9 *What I Remember*, [I], 376–377, 389, 505; II, 5–6, 23–24, 32, 37–39, 49; and Wright, *Life*, p. 320.

10 Sale number 349, item 197, Parke-Bernet Galleries, Inc., New York City, and Wright, *Life*, p. 320.

11 *What I Remember*, [I], 351–353, 360–361; Nonesuch *Letters*, III, 475–476 (see note 7, above); Wright, *Life*, p. 280, 320–321. Wright does not question the genuineness of Dickens' friendship for Frances Ternan Trollope.

12 *What I Remember*, II, 72–75, 137. Though the sister-in-law was not identified, it seems undoubtedly to have been Ellen, for, when mentioning Maria Ternan, Trollope gave her married name, Mrs. Rowland Taylor (ibid., II, 37).

13 Nonesuch *Letters*, III, 571. In the Memoranda Dickens said he would cable the day after his arrival, which would have been November 20. The cable was not received until November 22. Probably Dickens did not cable as soon as he had intended. He was in no hurry, for Wills was to transmit the message to Ellen by post.

The Ghost *at Brede Place*

♦

IT WAS DURING Stephen Crane's second residence in England, beginning in 1899, that he and his wife, Cora, made their home at Brede Place, just outside the village of Brede in East Sussex, seven miles west of Rye. "The old manor house . . . was loaned him by Mr. Frewen, the owner, and was built in the thirteenth century of almost porous stone," wrote an American friend of the Cranes', Karl Edwin Harriman, in an illustrated article in the *Critic* for July 1900. "The chill, damp, and draughts of the old house were terrible, believe me. The floors are of flagging, with great deceptive fireplaces, and the wind whistled through the casements every moment of the day and night." In *Mightier Than the Sword* Ford Madox Ford has colorfully described the "ill-fated mansion . . . in a damp hollow . . ., partly Elizabethan, partly even medieval . . ., full of evil influences. . . ."

In keeping with his manorial residence, Crane lived in a baronial sort of state at Brede Place. The house was generally full of company, some of it invited by the hospitable American and some self-invited. There was always food and drink for any passing wayfarer and for the stray dogs and lost cats which Ford remembered eating scraps beneath the dining table. Of course the house had ghosts. And the ghosts of Brede Place were sufficiently active to merit mention in a column in the *Saturday Evening Post* for July 28, 1900.

At Christmas time, 1899, the Cranes gave a large house party. Readers of reminiscences of Crane have long been aware that he and some of his friends produced a play of their own as part of the entertainment. In *Authors and I* Charles Lewis Hind (1862–1927), one of the guests, was perhaps the first to record his memories of the occasion:

> I received an invitation to spend three days in Brede Place; on the second day a play was to be performed at the schoolroom in Brede Village a mile away up the hill. This play we were informed, sub rosa, had been written by Henry James, H. G. Wells, A. E. W. Mason and other lights of literature.
>
> Duly I arrived at Brede Place. Surely there has never been such a house party. The ancient house, in spite of its size, was taxed to the uttermost. There were six men in the vast, bare chamber where I slept, the six iron bedsteads, procured for the occasion, quite lost in the amplitude of the chamber. At the dance, which was held on the evening of our arrival, I was presented to bevies of beautiful American girls in beauteous frocks....
>
> Of the play I have no recollection. The performance has been driven from my mind by the memory of the agony of getting to Brede village. It was a pouring wet night, with thunder and lightning. The omnibuses which transported us up the hill stuck in the miry roads. Again and again we had to alight and push, and

each time we returned to our seats on the top (the American girls were inside) I remarked to my neighbour, H. G. Wells, that Brede village is not a suitable place for dramatic performances.

H. G. Wells's recollections of the house party, recorded in *Experiment in Autobiography*, add little to Hind's. Mr. and Mrs. Wells, who were requested to bring their own bedding, arrived early and were fortunate to procure a room together. Wells spoke of "rehearsing a play vamped up by A. E. W. Mason, Crane, myself and others. It was a ghost play, and very allusive and fragmentary, and we gave it in the School Room at Brede. It amused its authors and caste vastly. What the Brede people made of it is not on record." Later Hind remembered it as "an awful play."

Although Crane's principal biographers have mentioned the little play, they have given no detailed account of it. Thomas Beer refers to it with characteristic obliqueness: "There were theatricals and the ghosts of Brede romped visibly." Calling the play by name, John Berryman enlarges upon "the main Brede ghost. This was a giant's ghost, sawn in two parts, of which Crane was fond." Crane's most recent bibliographers, Ames W. Williams and Vincent Starrett, seem sceptical of a "play supposedly written in collaboration with Joseph Conrad and others. Unpublished and manuscript probably lost."

The interest of the Berg Collection in the play was aroused several months ago when the Collection acquired a letter written by Crane to H. B. Marriott Watson from Brede Place on November 15, 1899: "We of Brede Place are giving a free play to the villagers at Christmas time in the school-house and I have written some awful rubbish which our friends will on that night speak out to the parish.

"But to make the thing historic, I have hit upon a plan of making the programmes choice by printing thereon a terrible list of authors of the comedy and to that end I have asked Henry James, Robert Barr, Joseph Conrad, A. E. W. Mason, H. G. Wells, Edwin Pugh, George Gissing, Rider Haggard and yourself to write a mere word – any word 'it', 'they', 'you', – any word and thus identify themselves with this crime.

"Would you be so lenient as to give me the word in your hand writing and thus appear in print on the programme with this distinguished rabble." At least a printed program had been planned – rendered choice by the array of collaborators.

By the greatest good luck the Berg Collection recently obtained the copy of the program of *The Ghost*. It had been presented to a Thomas Parkin by Cora Crane, who wrote Mr. Parkin in a letter postmarked January 29, 1900: "I also send you a program of the 'Ghost.' Its' a unique program. My husband sends you a copy of 'George's Mother.' You may like it as you appreciated 'Maggie.'" Mr. Parkin, who was a county magistrate and book collector living at Hastings, not far from Brede Place, annotated and grangerized his books. He laid the program of *The Ghost* into the copy of *George's Mother* which Crane had inscribed and presented to him and Mrs. Crane's letter and its accompanying envelope into his copy of *Maggie*. Both books are now in the Berg Collection.

The ten collaborators listed on the program of *The*

Ghost include at least half a dozen authors who are world famous: Henry James, George Gissing, Rider Haggard, Joseph Conrad, H. G. Wells, and Stephen Crane. The other four are not unknown. Robert Barr (1850–1912) was Scotland born, Canada reared, and trained in American journalism in Detroit. An accomplished editor and a successful writer of fiction, he collaborated with Crane on *The O'Ruddy*. Henry Brereton Marriott Watson (1863–1921) and Edwin William Pugh (1874–1930) both had some reputation as novelists. Alfred Edward Woodley Mason (1865–1948), who had been on the stage as a very young man, wrote popular novels and detective stories, of which *The Four Feathers* and *Königsmark* are still Hollywood perennials. Mason was the only collaborator who took part in the play, unless Mrs. H. G. Wells at the piano could be considered to represent her husband.

It is no surprise to discover among the dramatis personae allusions to characters in the works of some of the collaborators. Rufus Coleman is taken from Crane's *Active Service*. Doctor Moreau comes from H. G. Wells's *Island of Doctor Moreau*, and the doctor's son, Peter Quint Prodmore Moreau, is a hybrid, owing something also to Henry James's *Turn of the Screw* and perhaps to Joseph Conrad's *Nigger of the "Narcissus."* Suburbia may be an oblique reference to Edwin Pugh's *Street in Suburbia* and Tony Drunn to his *Tony Drum, Cockney Boy*. Miranda may derive from A. E. W. Mason's *Miranda of the Balcony* or H. B. Marriott Watson's *Heart of Miranda* or perhaps from both. Three Little Maids from Rye, Holly, Buttercup, and Mistletoe, are, if nothing more, at least an echo of *The Mikado*.

Fortunately Mr. Parkin inserted in his copy of *George's Mother* not only the program of *The Ghost* but a review of the play from the *Sussex Express, Surrey Standard, & Kent Mail* for Friday, January 5, 1900. It is headed "Brede. Mr. Stephen Crane Enlivens the Holidays," and is here quoted in full:

> On Thursday evening, December 28th, there was performed at the Brede Hill School-room, by an amateur company, an amusing little original play bearing the appropriate title of "The Ghost." The programme stated that the play was written by Messrs. Henry James, Robert Barr, George Gissing, Rider Haggard, Joseph Conrad, H. B. Marriott-Wilson, H. G. Wells, Edwin Pugh, A. E. W. Mason, and Stephen Crane, and it is a fact that all these notable authors had contributed something towards the libretto.
>
> The performers consisted of the Brede Place house party, assisted by a few friends, and Mr. Stephen Crane paid all the expenses incurred in producing the play. The children of the parish had attended a dress rehearsal on Wednesday afternoon, and on Thursday evening, in spite of the prevailing epidemic and bad weather, the room was filled by those who accepted Mr. Crane's invitations to see the performance.
>
> Mr. J. F. Smith had enlarged the existing stage, and had fixed up a correct proscenium. The back scene, which had been cleverly painted by Miss Richie, represented an empty room in Brede Place showing a realistic fire-place and chimney corner, and the wings gave a very good effect of bare walls.

The plot of the play was, shortly, as follows: – In the first act the ghost (Mr. A. E. W. Mason), in disguise, is discovered in the empty room in Brede Place in the year 1950; he soliloquises on ghosts and tourists in general, and upon himself and tourists to Brede – "children of Sussex East and West" – in particular. Two of the latter presently appear – Dr. Moreau (Mr. F. L. Bowen) and his son, Peter Quint Prodmore Moreau (Mr. Cunningham) – and converse with him. They are afterwards joined by the caretaker (Miss Bray), an historical story-teller, and the rest of the tourists. Three little maids from Rye – Holly (Mrs. Mark Barr), Buttercup (Miss Bowen), and Mistletoe (Miss Richie) – sing a trio. After this, while the other tourists are conducted off to the dining-room, "but not for lunch," Suburbia (Miss Ethel Bowen) and Miranda (Miss Sylvia Bowen) remain behind to get further information from their unknown companion about the ghost. Suburbia recites and Miranda dances, by way of recompensing the gentleman for his trouble. They learn that the ghost appears at midnight.

In the second act Rufus Coleman (Mr. Cyril Frewer) appears on the scene half an hour too early; he meets Mistletoe, who sings to him, telling how her lover has been the first to enlist in the Sussex volunteers against the Boers. After singing a duet they go out. There appear next in order Tony Drunn (Mr. Ford Richie), who sings the [sic] "The Soldiers of the Queen," and Dr. Moreau who, after some business with Tony Drunn, imitates some of the best known denizens of the farmyard, and sings "Simon the Cellarer." Holly joins him and sings at his request, and his son Peter makes his appearance. While the father and son are disputing as to who shall look after the young lady, Tony Drunn walks off with the latter. As the hour of midnight approaches, the tourists all return, and sing a chorus "We'll be there."

The third act – the program calls for only two – opens with a chorus "Oh, ghost, we're waiting for you to come," sung on the darkened stage. He soon appears and discloses his identity. He tells his story, supported by music, prompted by the caretaker, and helped out by the questions of the tourists. The play ends with a final chorus, in which the company sings the praises of Sir Goddard, their "wicked giant prize."

The songs, most of which were encored, were tastefully accompanied on the piano by Mrs. H. G. Wells. At the close of the performance a vote of thanks to the performers, proposed by Mr. Harvey, in the name of the Rector, who was absent through illness, was carried by acclamation. The audience sang "For they are jolly good people," the original word being changed in consideration of the ladies among those acting.

Perhaps some day a manuscript of *The Ghost* will turn up among the papers of one of the collaborators. If the text has disappeared forever, however, we know enough about it to rest assured that we have lost nothing more than a curiosity. Yet any curiosity that involved such an array of talent is a ghost that can never quite be laid.

A Legend Revisited:
Elinor Wylie

♦

"SHE WAS A LEGEND before she was a fact," Carl Van Doren wrote of Elinor Wylie after her death on December 15, 1928. Legends have a way of disappearing even from the scandal sheets of the national press that once made so free with her name. Changes in literary fashion have taken all but one of her four mannered novels out of print and obscured the power and beauty of the last of her four volumes of poetry, *Angels and Earthly Creatures*. The facts of her life, from which her poetry grew, were only imperfectly established in her sole biography, *The Portrait of an Unknown Lady*, 1935, by her younger sister, the novelist Nancy Hoyt. Yet her story has the fascination of classical tragedy, and a reexamination of literary values will inevitably bring her work back to public attention.

The legend of Elinor Wylie is recorded in the work and in the reminiscences of her friends and enemies, eminent figures of the 1920s. She is sympathetically delineated by Kathleen Coyle in *Immortal Ease* as Victoria Rising and by Isa Glenn in *East of Eden* as Eva Littlefeld. Nancy Hoyt treated her frivolously as Athene in *Bright Intervals* and Anne Parrish maliciously as Christable Caine in *All Kneeling*. She described herself with a detachment remarkable for her temperament in a long poem wittily entitled "Portrait in Black Paint, with a Very Sparing Use of Whitewash." To her memory Edna St. Vincent Millay, ever her champion, dedicated *Fatal Interview* in 1931.

The quality allowed her in varying degrees by both admirers and detractors is beauty. Kathleen Norris, the American novelist, who was a hostile witness, admitted that had it not been for "an expression of faint discontent about her mouth and a restless use of the eyes that were always looking for something else," Elinor Wylie "might have been quite beautiful, with her colorless clear-cut face, superb dark eyes that were framed by a great mop of curled dark hair. . . ." Edith Olivier, the English novelist, recalled in "Concerning Elinor Wylie" her first vivid impression of the poet: "She was wearing a dress made of stiff, shiny silk, and it looked like frozen green water. She was tall . . . holding herself very erect, with a smooth evenness of carriage. . . . Her face was heart-shaped, and very white, and the copper-colored hair curved nobly away from the sides of her forehead."

Miss Olivier's description implies the distinction of person that her admirers have also commented on, a grace of personality that she retained when gracelessness was widely fashionable. She loved elegant clothes, which she bought in Paris when she could afford them. She felt at her best in a silver dress created for her by a dressmaker famous in the 1920s, Paul Poiret. She had a passion for silver in clothes, in jewelry, in household furnishings. Wherever she lived, she contrived an aristocratic atmosphere of taste, of refinement. Frank Crowninshield, editor of *Vanity Fair*, pointed out that she liked "to pretend she was a Bohemian but the sham was at all times apparent." Her third husband, the poet William Rose Benét, wrote after her death: "The fastidiousness that Elinor Wylie brought to her art was reflected in every worldly possession and in every gesture of her life."

The great exception to this well-nigh universal admission is Virginia Woolf's description of the poet in a letter to Vita Sackville-West:

Oh what an evening! I expected a ravishing and diaphanous dragon fly, a woman who had spirited away four husbands . . . a Siren; a green and sweet voiced nymph – that was what I expected, and came a tiptoe into the room to find – a solid hunk: a hatchet minded, cadaverous, acid voiced, bare boned, spavined, patriotic nasal, thick legged American. All the evening she declaimed unimpeachable truths; and discussed our sales: hers are three times better than mine, naturally; till, thank God, she began a-heaving on her chair and made a move as if to go, gracefully yielded to, but not, I beg you to believe, solicited, on our parts. Figure my woe, on the stairs, when she murmured, "It's the other thing I want. Comes of trying to have children. May I go in there?" So she retired to the W.C., emerged refreshed; sent away her cab, and stayed another hour, hacking us to pieces. But I must read *The Venetian Glass Nephew*.

Not only was Elinor Wylie generally acknowledged to be a beauty; many considered her a genius. In *Three Worlds* Carl Van Doren coupled her beauty and genius.

Doubly endowed, she was "doubly driven. She was one of
the most arresting women of this or any age." Benét un-
equivocally called her a "genius." Others, like Edmund
Wilson, were ready to concede the extraordinary variety of
her intellectual gifts. She was a poet and a novelist, with a
scholar's energy and thoroughness in research. "Like many
women who have suffered, she had her moments of serious
unbalance," Mary Colum recorded in *Life and the Dream*,
"but what really stood to her was her industry at her work
and the discipline that came with it. She had made herself
. . . an intellectual and a scholar."

Some of the spell of Elinor Wylie's personality lay in
her talk, which brought into play the power and charm of
her unusual mind. She had had the example and tutelage of
Horace Wylie, who was, she once declared, "the most fascinating conversationalist" she ever knew. Burton Rascoe,
the critic and editor, who allowed her "genius," found her
conversation more suggestive of the eighteenth century she
loved than of twentieth-century New York. "Her talk . . .
had both style and wit," Edmund Wilson remembered.

Such gifts are rarely unaccompanied by vanity, which
friend and foe alike found pervasive in Elinor Wylie's character. "She was one of the most beautiful women I have
ever known and the vainest," Louis Untermeyer stated can-
didly in *From Another World*. "She was vain about the merit
for which she was least responsible, her physical beauty."
Edith Olivier called her "the most egotistical person I ever
knew. . . . She enjoyed nothing more than a serious discussion of her own personal appearance." Even her admirer
Carl Van Doren confessed that it was "boring . . . she could

never bear being less than first in any company." Mary
Colum deplored "the vanity she could never conceal or
camouflage. . . . If she was not overtly considered the most
important and beautiful person in every gathering, she suffered and showed her suffering openly." Yet Rebecca West
gave a charitable explanation: ". . . much that struck the
superficial observer as egotism was an unbridled passion for
perfection too thorough-going to exempt herself from praise
or blame."

Her vanity, unhappily, produced what the admiring
James Branch Cabell described in *As I Remember It* as a
"touchiness beyond instant belief, alike as to her writings,
every least line of them, and her personal loveliness also. . . .
From her associates she required continuous flattery." Cabell recalled that although he had been "loud-lunged in
praise of her first two romances," he had found *The Orphan
Angel* "impenetrable." Thereupon Elinor Wylie, as he put
it, "dropped his acquaintance." This touchiness, also commented on by the Colums and Edmund Wilson, led to
public scenes. Once, Carl Van Doren recollected, feeling
herself neglected at an evening party at Theodore Dreiser's,
she forced her friends to follow her into another room to
listen to her recite some of her poetry. Once she left Kathleen Norris' dinner table and "flung herself upon a bed,
raging because some innocent guest had observed that G. B.
Stern was the most important woman writer of the day."

According to Carl Van Vechten in *Fragments from an
Unwritten Autobiography*, she was

> a warm, generous person but friendship with her had
> to be on her own terms. . . . She was a great writer and

a great beauty: nothing less would do. . . . At the slightest sign of rebellion . . . Elinor would dissolve into tears. Vanity asks for flattery, in fact demands it, and her whole life and career, amorous, artistic and commercial, was based on flattery, an attention she exacted in exchange for her friendship and confidence. It was not difficult to give her. She was handsome, if not beautiful, and what she did in writing she did superlatively.

Even Benét, describing Elinor as Sylvia in *The Dust Which Is God*, admitted somewhat unpoetically: "Sylvia . . . could be difficult as hell sometimes/but never (by her values) a pain in the neck/although upon occasion a corruscation of lightning a sudden blinding thunderbolt."

The most unfavorable view of her personality in print was taken by Kathleen Norris, the novelist and sister of the first Mrs. William Rose Benét. The principal source of her dislike seems to have been that Elinor Wylie was a bad stepmother to Teresa Benét's three children, who did ultimately go to live on the West Coast with their Norris relatives. Mrs. Norris was impatient with Elinor, who, after breaking up two families by her elopement with Horace Wylie, insisted upon her love of children and was "endlessly argumentative" about the legality and morality of her three marriages "even in Catholic eyes."

Nobody was worrying about these points or even discussing them, but she could not leave them alone. . . . We all make curious mistakes in self-analysis, but hers was tragic; trying to reconcile her actual character and her destiny with what she wanted and hoped them to be, and yet knew they were not, kept her spirit in a state of continual unrest. . . . In fact, despite beauty, brains, youth, with a talent close to genius, and fame, she was troublesome. Three men – one might say men of distinction – had married her – and many others had indicated their admiration in unmistakable terms, but "dissatisfied" was the word that inevitably was fitted to her, and everyone who knew her wondered what on earth she wanted.

Kathleen Norris was not alone in her reading of Elinor Wylie's face. Edmund Wilson noticed her discontent and rebellion. The English novelist Rose Macaulay, meeting her in the late 1920s, described her as "the most unhappy looking woman [she] had ever seen." They all may have overlooked the effect of poor vision on her expression: she should have worn the spectacles her vanity would not permit.

To offset her vanity Elinor Wylie possessed what her admirers considered a rare degree of courage. "She worshipped courage," Benét declared. "She herself had suffered deeply, and still suffered proudly from early recklessness." The sufferings exacted a physical as well as a spiritual toll. During the last fifteen years of her life she endured what he referred to as "almost constant physical pain" from high blood pressure, essential hypertension, and hemocranial headaches. Her physician for her last five years, Dr. Connie Guion, remembers her endurance and humor in the face of pain. Padraic and Mary Colum were both impressed by her bravery, "physical as well as spiritual." In Mrs. Colum's words, Elinor Wylie had "learned a great deal from living," including "a despair which seemed to be another name for courage and combat." She could meet anguish of body and mind, heart and spirit with "a fine, steely courage." The opposite point of view was dispassionately expressed by Sara Teasdale: "She seemed heroic if you liked her, hysterical if you didn't."

Upon a few Elinor Wylie made a really sinister impression. Padraic Colum, who admired her appearance and her literary gifts, thought her a "dangerous" person of whom to make a friend. She was too mercurial to be trusted. A friend of the Benét family described her as "the only evil person" she ever knew. Both sources recollect unpleasantly her whim of sending Benét, who just before the marriage was staying with his parents, a telegram breaking their engagement – with the sole intention of shocking his mother.

Behind the legend lie the facts that made Elinor Hoyt Hichborn Wylie Benét the woman she was. The first Hoyt settled in Massachusetts in 1629 and her branch of the family – from whom she inherited what she called "the johnny-cake" or country folk side of her character – lived in Pennsylvania from the late eighteenth century. Her grandfather Henry Martyn Hoyt, raised to farm life, was a brigadier general in the Civil War, a judge, and governor of Pennsylvania. Her father, also Henry Martyn Hoyt, was in the class of 1878 at Yale. After success at the Pennsylvania bar he received federal appointments as assistant attorney general in 1897 and as solicitor general in 1903. In 1883 he married Anne McMichael and had five children, of whom the eldest, born September 7, 1885, was christened Elinor Morton.

The McMichaels were of Irish descent. The child's
great-great-grandfather had worked on the estate of Joseph
Bonaparte in Bordentown, New Jersey. Her great-grand-
father rose to be a lawyer, politician, and man of letters in
Philadelphia, editing the *Saturday Evening Post* and the *North
American Review*. Her grandfather went into banking and
amassed a sizable fortune.

Elinor Hoyt was especially close to the men among her
progenitors. She was devoted to her grandfather McMichael, who took her to Europe in 1903 to show her the
great world. She felt a passionate admiration for her father,
who is remembered as an attractive, warm-hearted, and in-
telligent man by a childhood friend of Elinor's, who recalls
Mrs. Hoyt as a psychosomatic invalid much addicted to the
sofa. She could do little with her children and, according to
Mary Colum, contributed to the vanity of her eldest by
calling attention to the beautiful hair of her "lion child" –
an expression that stuck in Hoyt phraseology. During some
unfortunate family incident, she exclaimed, "I have given
birth to a generation of vipers!" Unstable they certainly
were: one son and one daughter killed themselves and another son survived jumping off a liner in mid-Atlantic.

As a girl Elinor Hoyt had the experiences that went
with her social, financial, and political connections in Philadelphia and Washington. She went to the Baldwin School,
in Bryn Mawr, and to Holton Arms in the capital. She
spent her summers on Mount Desert, with noticeable effect
on the imagery of her poetry. She was always a great
reader. She "wrote"; she studied drawing and painting. At
eighteen she made her debut and for a bluestocking was

much admired. She had, according to Nancy Hoyt, an unsuccessful love affair with a suitable young man. It may have induced – in 1903–4 – the first of the four periods in her life when she was absorbed in writing poetry. It may be the fact behind the story that she married Hichborn in 1905 on the rebound.

Philip Simmons Hichborn was almost exactly three years his wife's senior. His father had risen from shipwright's apprentice to rear admiral in the Construction Corps. The boy was in the class of 1905 at Harvard, where he belonged to the right clubs and the *Lampoon*. He wrote sporting stories of some competence, published in *Hoof Beats* by a Boston vanity press in 1912, and romances of which Elinor was the heroine. Hichborn was described by his sister-in-law as a "nice-looking and well-born young suitor with a bad temper."

From the beginning the marriage seems to have been unhappy, and Elinor remained dependent upon her family, especially upon her father. The birth of a son, Philip III, on September 22, 1907, did not strengthen the relationship of the young Hichborns. Then in 1910 a series of psychological blows brought the marriage down. On May 1, 1910, Admiral Hichborn died, followed on November 20 by Mr. Hoyt. Elinor Hichborn lost the support of the relationship with an older man that seems always to have been essential to her emotional well-being. On December 16 she eloped with Horace Wylie, some sixteen years her senior.

In fact, Wylie may have been seventeen years older than Elinor: according to conflicting Yale records, he was born on September 16, 1868 or more likely 1869. His father was Judge Andrew Wylie of the Supreme Court of the District of Columbia. Horace Wylie was an editor of the Yale *Record* and a member of the class of 1889. He took his degree at the Harvard University Law School in 1892 and was admitted to the bar of the District of Columbia the same year. The Wylies were wealthy: the family fortune was estimated at a million dollars. The young man was able to go around the world in 1894 before his marriage on April 30, 1895, to Katherine Virginia Hopkins, daughter of James H. Hopkins, a member of the House of Representatives from Pittsburgh. By 1910 they had had six children, two of whom died in infancy. Wylie was described by the newspaper as "handsome . . . full faced, broad shouldered, diffident in manner and extremely courteous and affable." The gossip columns chattered that before Elinor there had been another young woman for whom he had left Mrs. Wylie but that after a month he had returned to his wife, who "served notice that never again would she stand for such an escapade."

Mary Colum's impression of him, derived from Elinor, emphasizes in a negative way the need and preference for older men that mark the poet's emotional relationships. But she adds, "From what I have heard of him from others, Horace Wylie was neither so interesting, so brilliant nor such a man of the world as Elinor believed him to be; she was highly impressed by people, men or women, whom she believed to be *du monde*, and delighted in the phrase 'persons of quality.'" Mrs. Colum believed that Elinor's romantic notions of Horace were nearer the truth than the deprecating description of him that he was "dull and uninteresting" or that he "had the mind of a suburban realtor."

News of the elopement broke in the press on December 22, and from that moment on Elinor was never free from the sting of notoriety. A few sentences quoted from several issues of *Town Topics*, a defunct scandal sheet, illustrate the persecution to which she was to be subjected:

Intimates of the Hichborn family know that since Mrs. Hichborn's father died about two months ago, she has not been at all the same. . . . She seemed to take a dislike to society and frequently denied herself to her most intimate friends. Those who saw her in the last few weeks declare that she was on the verge of a nervous breakdown. . . . It has become known that Philip Hichborn and his wife did not get along together, as she was high-spirited and fun-loving, while he was inclined to be studious and rather silent at most times. The matrimonial breach between them was widened a good deal last Summer say some of their friends, and it is told by women who were there that after an unusually heavy row the young wife vowed that she would make away with herself in the lake.

The pair went to England in the winter of 1911. In April Elinor sent Horace back to Mrs. Wylie for a five-months' trial reconciliation to prove that the elopement was more than an "escapade." Perhaps Elinor knew of the earlier episode in Horace Wylie's life and needed reassurance. While she remained with her mother, Horace and Katherine Wylie and the four children left at the end of May on a long trip to Europe. The Hichborn ladies made Philip Hichborn, who was willing to take back his errant wife, according to a statement he later released to the press, wait six months before doing so. The newspapers erupted with rumors that Elinor had been jilted and had had a complete breakdown. Then on September 26, 1911, Elinor and Horace abandoned their families a second and last time and joined each other. Wylie settled two-thirds of his estate – estimated at $300,000 – on his wife and children.

For almost five years Mrs. Wylie refused to divorce her husband. On January 6, 1912, however, Philip Hichborn, the abandoned husband, brought action in the Supreme Court of the District of Columbia naming Horace as corespondent. But before the petition was heard Hichborn, aged twenty-nine, blew his brains out on March 27, 1912, at the house of his sister, Mrs. Paul Pearsall. He left a note attributing to ill health this violent solution to all mortal problems, but the general belief was that grief caused by the loss of his wife was the reason. Elinor seems to have felt her responsibility: she never ceased trying to convince herself and her friends that the elopement had had nothing to do with the suicide because the bullet was fired eighteen months later. Mrs. Pearsall adopted young Philip, her nephew, then some four and a half years old, and it was probably for the custody of the boy that the divorce of the dead man was pushed through to the end.

Until July 1916 Elinor Hichborn and Horace Wylie lived in England as Mr. and Mrs. Waring. Elinor was extremely anxious to have children, regardless of their legal status, and suffered more than one miscarriage. Early in their life together, in 1910–12, she became absorbed a second time in writing poetry, perhaps stimulated by her feeling for Horace. Her slight first volume of verses, *Incidental Numbers*, was privately printed in London in 1912 at Horace Wylie's expense.

The Warings lived more or less pseudonymously in many different places in England, with visits to the Continent. The First World War introduced the need for identification papers, which put an official end to the fiction of the Warings. Fortunately for them, Mrs. Wylie, to obtain custody of her children, petitioned for divorce early in July 1916. Horace and Elinor returned to Boston where they were married on August 7, 1916, almost six years after their first elopement.

Their official marriage lasted some months longer than six years. Elinor Wylie's petition for divorce from Horace Wylie on grounds of nonsupport was provisionally granted in Rhode Island on March 26, 1923 – the next day was the eleventh anniversary of Philip Hichborn's death – and confirmed on October 1, 1923. During their six years of marriage they lived together in Boston, on Mount Desert, in Augusta, Georgia, and in Washington. Horace Wylie was no longer affluent and took a traveling position with the Interstate Commerce Commission at some $100 a month. Elinor began writing again in 1918 poetry of a far more mature and finished quality than any she had yet achieved, poetry that she was to bring rapidly to an extraordinary technical perfection. This third period of poetic activity lasted until 1924 – the half-dozen years that were also marked by her resumption of the legal position of a married woman and the disintegration of her marriage with Horace Wylie. Elinor never discussed the reasons for the change even with so close a friend as Carl Van Doren. Horace Wylie is reported to have counseled: "You had better remain with me, Elinor. You are a fantastic creature and I understand you." But in 1921 Elinor settled in New York at 1 University Place, then one of the old houses facing the Square, and saw her first published collection of poems, *Nets to Catch the Wind*, achieve a wide critical success. Although Horace Wylie was no longer necessary to her, she never ceased to use him as a standard and to seek in other men the qualities which she admired in him.

In May 1927 she wrote to him from London:

Dearest Horace,

A strange thing is going to happen to you, for that thing is going to come true which undoubtedly you once desired, & for which you will now not care a straw. I am going to admit to you that I wish with all my heart I had never left you. I don't want you to keep this letter, & I hope – & trust – that you will tell no one, but although the admission may afford us both a certain pain, it is founded upon such deep principles of truth & affection that I feel it should be made.

You must not tell this, because the knowledge of it would give pain to Bill, who is one of the best people who ever lived & with whom I expect to pass the remainder of my days. But you & I know that that remainder is not long, & the entire past – which is so much longer – makes me wish to tell you the truth.

I love you, Horace, with an unchanged love which is far more than friendship, & which will certainly persist until my death. It is impossible for me to tell your present sentiments towards me, but it can hardly be a matter for regret that your former devotion should have bred a devotion in me which nothing could destroy. . . .

Well, my dear, do not think I am divorcing Bill or something like that. He is the best boy imaginable. I suppose it is, in a way, churlish to write this. But I loved you first, I loved you more, I loved him afterwards, but now, that I love you both, I love you best. Surely you must, in some way, be glad to know this.

Mary Colum believed that Horace Wylie dominated her taste to the very end of her life. He survived her until December 28, 1950, when he died of a stroke in Washington, leaving a widow whose maiden name had been Eleanor Taylor.

In 1920, Elinor Wylie had renewed her friendship with the man who was to become her third husband. William Rose Benét had been a close friend of her brother Henry Hoyt in the class of 1907 at Yale. Her brother, an artist of considerable talent, had been left by his wife after the war, and Benét had lost his wife in the flu epidemic in January 1919. Henry Hoyt had been the closest to Elinor of her own generation in her family and, like Philip Hichborn, he was to kill himself, certainly in part over the failure of his marriage. He shared a studio apartment in New York with Benét and died more or less in Benét's arms in August 1920 at the age of thirty-three. The tragedy had thrown Elinor and Benét together, and he, five months her junior, had quickly fallen in love.

Benét immediately recognized the extraordinary quality of her poetry and encouraged her to treat her gift with
high seriousness. Their relationship deepened over the preparation of her second collection of poems, *Black Armour*,
published by George H. Doran in the spring of 1923, and
of her first novel, *Jennifer Lorn*, which Doran published
that autumn. Colonel and Mrs. James W. Benét, the groom's
parents, were greatly distressed by the impending marriage.
The Colonel even went to Europe in order to be excused
from attending the ceremony.

Elinor Wylie and Benét were married on October 5,
1923, four days after her divorce became final. They were
both professional writers, he the less successful of the two.
During their married life of five years Benét produced three
books – poems, essays, and a children's story – and Elinor
three novels – *The Venetian Glass Nephew* in 1925, *The Orphan Angel* in 1926, and *Mr. Hodge and Mr. Hazard* in 1928
– and two collections of poetry, *Trivial Breath* also in 1928,
and *Angels and Earthly Creatures*, posthumously published
in 1929. This rounds out her extraordinary record of four
novels and four volumes of verse in eight years, to say
nothing of the other poems published long after her death
in *Collected Poems*, 1932, and *Last Poems*, 1943, and the "Fu-
gitive" pieces in the *Collected Prose*, 1933. At the beginning
of their marriage they were hard up, despite the continua-
tion of the allowance that Elinor had received from her
mother for about a decade. Her health, furthermore, had
been uncertain for the same length of time but she refused
to take care of herself. She longed for children and never

ceased to feel guilty over having abandoned her son. "I left my baby when I ran away. That is the only thing I have ever done that I can think was bad," she admitted to Carl Van Doren. "And now I would rather have a child that I could think of as really my own than anything else I could really have." She did not see Philip, her son, from 1910 to 1918 and after that only intermittently, although they are reported to have had a natural attraction toward each other. In her marriage with Benét the history of miscarriages was repeated. Only a few months before her death she wrote him: "It is, and always will be, the greatest tragedy and complete frustration of my life that I am childless."

From 1922 to 1925, she went to the MacDowell Colony at Peterborough, New Hampshire, to obtain the repose that enabled her to produce her amazing output. In the summer of 1926 she made her first trip alone to England. Her inherited love of England had been fostered during her life there with Horace Wylie. Since she was a girl, her attendant spirit had been an English poet, Shelley, and her relationship with him had seemed so real, so compensatory for her emotional failures, that in the opinion of Carl Van Doren it actually interfered with her feelings for living men. Now she made new friends and through one friendship she experienced the emotion that led to the writing of her finest poetry. This friend was the man to whom she dedicated *Angels and Earthly Creatures: A Sequence of Sonnets*, as these great sonnets of love and renunciation were originally called when privately printed at Henley in 1928, and later "One Person" when they were included in the posthumous volume *Angels and Earthly Creatures*. This collection contained

the work of her fourth and final period of poetic activity in
1927–28 under the impetus of a new love. William Rose
Benét has left a slightly disguised version of this relationship
in *The Dust Which Is God*. The most factual accounts of it
can be found in the reminiscences of Carl Van Doren and
Mary Colum.

When Elinor first read the sonnets to Van Doren in
London in the summer of 1928, she told him that she had
met a man

> whom at last she loved absolutely. . . . She had never
> been in love before, she was sure. She had only been
> loved. . . . Little enough had actually come of it. Jealous
> circumstances had kept the lovers apart. . . . Little
> enough could ever come of it. She would not disrupt
> her life again. This must remain a radiant experience of
> the mind. But it did not belong solely to her mind. It
> was flesh, too, and it tore at her. She cried out against
> the cruel separation. "I don't want much. I don't ex-
> pect it. I could be satisfied if I could know that some-
> time, maybe when we are very old, we could spend
> the night under one roof. It would not have to be to-
> gether. Only under the same roof, peacefully."

Her description of the new beloved did not impress Van
Doren, although the intensity of her emotion did: "To me,
she did not make him sound glorious, though she tried. All
the glory was in her." The only expression of their love was
apparently in the sonnets. "This final love had come to her
like first love," Van Doren observed, and in the sonnets
"the heart of sixteen spoke with the tongue of forty."

Only two days before her death in New York Elinor

showed Mary Colum, who had first heard the sonnets the
previous night, a snapshot of the man who had inspired
them –

> a tallish-looking, obviously middle-aged man [Mrs.
> Colum observed]. That she was really in love with this
> man I believe to be true and real as far as romantic love
> is reality. . . . "I am not taking anything on this time,"
> she said, and these are her words precisely. "He calls to
> see me once a week, and we talk, (a great deal about
> philosophy), and sometimes walk together". . . . As
> she spoke to me of it, it seemed a simple and rather
> pathetic relationship where two people with obliga-
> tions to others were attracted to each other in a roman-
> tic and intellectual way. Elinor seemed to be attached
> to his family and spoke of them with affection.

Mary Colum provides further evidence that in this new
love Elinor turned to someone who, like Horace Wylie,
represented to her the older man, provider of stability and
strength like her adored father.

> As she showed me his photograph she said, "I think
> he is like Horace Wylie – You would have liked Hor-
> ace." I began to think that maybe it was all somehow
> the continuation of the thread of her life with Horace
> Wylie . . . her life in the English country once more
> . . . the visits to London . . . the old life she had once
> told me about relived again almost as in a dream.

Although many have spoken of this man in print, no
one so far has given him a name. In the Benét correspondence at Yale, however, is evidence of his identity that is
corroborated by details in *The Dust Which Is God* and in

Nancy Hoyt's biography of her sister. Elinor met Henry de Clifford Woodhouse of Rockylane Farm, Rotherfield Greys, Oxfordshire, near Henley-on-Thames, his wife, Becky, and their children on her visit to England in 1926. Her feeling for Woodhouse reached full flower in the summer of 1928, when she spent much time in Henley at the Old Cottage, and the flowering can be found in the love sonnets and the metaphysical poems in *Angels and Earthly Creatures.*

At the Woodhouses' Elinor experienced her first stroke, when she thought she had merely fainted and fallen down nine steps. She forced herself to rise, despite the pain in her back, and joined the others in the garden because she felt that Mrs. Woodhouse thought her "spoiled and even cowardly." She made little of the fall and the Woodhouses let her go back to London on the train alone. It proved an agonizing journey. She had "dislocated and injured a vertebra half way down her spine" and had fractured the end of her spine.

Apparently Elinor did not tell Benét of her new absorption until he joined her in England in the middle of the summer of 1928. He, too, met the Woodhouses, of whom he naturally took a mixed view. He expressed his own resentment by bitterly singling out what he considered their callousness about her accident. Yet he tried to give his rival his due. "I liked the man as a casual acquaintance – aside from the present situation," he wrote Elinor on his way back to New York early in September. If Elinor found goodness in Cliff, he would not deny it. "As to matters of the heart," he conceded, "what you perceive you perceive and I have never known you to perceive goodness and be at fault." He was apparently convinced that the love was unconsummated and he felt that the very demand for self-sacrifice caught Elinor's imagination. He wrote her from the *Homeric*: "Your heart is supremely governed – it was notably so in my case – by your pity, your maternal feeling, your desire for a romantic abnegation. . . . This appeal to your sympathy seems to me, frankly, to have been rather blatant and weak." He generously admitted, "I am sure he loves you. So does this wretched Bill." "I hope to live with you," he insisted, "so long as you still wish to live with me."

Benét would hardly have been human if he had never – even by implication – compared Woodhouse adversely to himself. "Only," he pointed out, "when I heard the object of extravagant abasement in immortal sonnets, ejaculate 'What does it mean?' blankly of a simple ballad, and say nothing at all to one of the greatest mystical poems of our time delivered with the true poetic frenzy, – I can but ponder again on the frequent occurrence in life of the love of the star for the void." Nancy Hoyt, too, who had ample opportunity to meet Woodhouse at Henley and who mentions him, but not by name, deprecated Elinor's enthusiasms and "shining lights. For they were usually just quite ordinary every-day people on whom the beam of her wild unbounded admiration would fall. . . . Elinor had no illusions about the mental attainments of her pets; it was that they were different from other mortals, of finer clay, even when they were a little bit stupid."

The autumn of 1928 seems to have brought some estrangement between Elinor and Woodhouse. Shortly after

Benét left England she referred to the Woodhouses in a letter to him as "a pair of heavy cotton blankets soaked in bilge-water." Possibly her vanity had been wounded because Woodhouse accepted her abnegation too willingly. By early October the wound was apparently healing. "I am *glad*, awfully *glad*," Benét wrote her, "if Woodlice have proved human." Nancy Hoyt insisted that a few days before her death Elinor told her "about her waning admiration for a gentleman in England. . . ." In the first letter of condolence which Becky Woodhouse wrote on December 20, 1928, an estrangement is implied by her protestation: "Surely you can no longer doubt that we loved her, Bill."

From this difficult situation Becky Woodhouse emerges as one of those remarkable women with an understanding heart and a generous mind, and Cliff comes out with credit. On January 30, 1929, Mrs. Woodhouse wrote Benét again. "I think that in this last book is to be found the finest flower of all her work. I think, dear Bill, that she guessed – or I hope she did – that I understood – for her real gift to me at Christmas was an exquisitely bound copy of the sonnets." A few days later Woodhouse wrote Benét a letter that helps to explain Elinor's feeling for him. "I know that Elinor loved us both very much indeed and I also know that she attributed to me qualities which I don't possess and only wish that I did. Her imagination, I think, ran away with her. . . . Dear old man Bill, know that I feel it a great honour to have shared some of the great affection your Elinor had for you."

Many years later in 1962 Mrs. Woodhouse confirmed her feelings about Elinor to the present author:

You obviously do not know what an effort it cost me to let you come here. . . . I am not attempting to dramatize a situation which is hackneyed enough. But I *do* want you to understand just why I want to shut the door again and to recapture something of the peace of mind and understanding we've reached in old age. . . . In all fairness to Cliff I must add that Elinor did pursue him relentlessly and would not take NO.

When Elinor returned to New York in early December 1928 she planned to return to England in mid-January 1929, in order to be in the same country as Woodhouse, she told Mary Colum. She did not know that she had suffered a second stroke in October 1928. It had affected her face and had been diagnosed as Bell's paralysis. She wanted to see Benét, with whom she stayed in their apartment at 36 West 9th Street, and prepare the copy for the publication of *Angels and Earthly Creatures* by Knopf. The task was completely finished on December 15. The next day was the eighteenth anniversary of her elopement with Horace Wylie. It was also the day of her death. She suffered a third and fatal stroke.

The dramatic account that Benét gives in *The Dust Which Is God* is undoubtedly accurate. He heard her call out for a glass of water and took it into the room where he had left her reading the sermons of John Donne. He saw her standing by her chair and starting to move toward him. "What is it?" he asked and she replied, "I don't – know," and fell at his feet. She never regained consciousness.

Note

Permission to publish from unpublished letters was graciously granted by Mrs. Barnet Rubinstein, Elinor Wylie's niece, Mrs. J. Crawford Ware, daughter of Mr. and Mrs. Henry de Clifford Woodhouse, and Mr. Leonard Woolf; and by the Beinecke Rare Book and Manuscript Library of Yale University and the Berg Collection of The New York Public Library.

Carl Van Vechten

*Notes for an Exhibition in Honor of
His Seventy-fifth Birthday*

◆

FOR NEARLY HALF A CENTURY Carl Van Vechten has been a familiar and potent figure in the artistic and intellectual life of New York. Few others in his own or any other generation in the literary history of this country have had so many diverse talents and have brought them to such successful fruition. Few others have been so generous in calling attention to the talents of other individuals and groups.

Beginning as a newspaper reporter, Mr. Van Vechten became a music and drama critic to reckon with. His work in these fields was not lost in the files of periodicals; it was revised and, in permanent form, reached a wide audience of book readers. Reversing the usual procedure, he next made a name for himself as a novelist – one whose stories were acclaimed as the expression of sophisticated New York in the 1920s. Finally he has achieved a high reputation as a photographer of the personalities of the theatre, the ballet, music, and literature. Most of the subjects of his photographs have been his friends, and he has been tireless in directing notice to their work in his own books, in periodicals, and in introductions to books they themselves have written.

Mr. Van Vechten's seventy-fifth birthday provides a

fitting occasion for admirers of the man and his work to testify to the broadening of their horizons and the pleasure which his abilities and his energy have given them. The New York Public Library is fortunate in the interest which he has taken in its many collections. As the recipient of Mr. Van Vechten's literary papers and memorabilia, it is indeed happy in being able to share a selection of these with the public by means of an exhibition for which the following notes were prepared.

THE YOUTH

Many years after the event, Carl Van Vechten was to celebrate in an essay the advantages of having been born on his particular birthday, the seventeenth of June. The year was 1880. The place was Cedar Rapids, Iowa. The first Van Vechten to come to this country settled on a farm opposite what is now Albany, New York, in 1638. Mr. Van Vechten's mother's people, the Fitches, also came from New York State. When he later took New York City as his province, he was really returning to the world of his ancestors. The progress of his forebears had been gradually westward; his own was to be as steadily eastward.

The earliest of the photographs shown in the exhibition reveals the author at the age of ten months, as carefully posed against a flowered shawl as he would later pose some of the celebrated subjects of his own photographs. The comfortable-looking house was built in 1881 for his father, and here the boy lived until he went away to college nearly two decades later.

Charles Duane Van Vechten, the father, dominates a photograph of the family group despite the height of his son Ralph, then twenty-one years old, and despite his pretty daughter of sixteen, Emma, who stand behind him. Going west from New York in 1855, the father had become a successful insurance broker and banker, a profession in which his son Ralph successfully followed him. Leaning against his mother, Ada Amanda Fitch Van Vechten, is Carl, aged three, a latecomer to the family. Another photograph – of a serious small boy with large brown eyes – is easily recognized as a portrait of the artist as a man of eight.

From his earliest days Carl Van Vechten was drawn to the theatre and to writing. While he was a pupil at Cedar Rapids High School, he wrote and acted in plays, a notable success being his adaptation of *The Prisoner of Zenda*, in which he scored in the part of the villain. His ambitions to be a playwright died slowly and were buried in the manuscripts of several unsuccessful dramas worked out over the ensuing decades.

After graduating from Cedar Rapids High in January 1899, he made his first move toward the East. He obtained a Ph.B. degree from the University of Chicago in 1903. There he was a student of Robert Morss Lovett's, who became a life-long friend. Among the Van Vechten papers are numerous college themes with comments in Lovett's hand. The young man enjoyed the social as well as the literary side of college life: he was a member of Psi Upsilon and a steady contributor to the *University of Chicago Weekly*.

The earliest known appearance of Carl Van Vechten in print can be found in the copy of the Cedar Rapids High

School magazine, the *Pulse*, for October 1901. In "Alumni Correspondence" he reports on the excitement and disillusionment of being rushed for a college fraternity.

His first known contribution to the *University of Chicago Weekly*, January 9, 1902, was "Love Me, Love My Dog," a tale of the social complexities of fraternities and sororities, with a garnishing of romance. The urge to create was persistent and though his productions were routine, he had the ability to make literary use of the life around him.

THE JOURNALIST

In the issue of the *Pulse* for January 1904, Mr. Van Vechten, now a graduate of the University of Chicago and a cub reporter for Hearst's *Chicago American*, reported to Cedar Rapids High School the events of his Thanksgiving Day, 1903, assignment for the paper. He had covered the Harrison Street police station, where he found good copy in a Negro prisoner with delirium tremens – "yet not a bad Thanksgiving." It was natural that he should turn to newspaper work after graduating and natural that he should enjoy it. It was a good school for the future novelist.

But all his writing was not journalistic. To this period belong some of the juvenilia through which he was learning his way around other literary forms besides the news-story.

Some of Carl Van Vechten's work for the *Chicago American* involved filling a gossip column under the anonym of "The Chaperon." Though such chatter probably sharpened the edge of his social satire, fortunately he was not confined to the society page. He worked in many different departments of the paper – once, indeed, getting up "a baby show which was so big a success they had to call the police!" He remained with Hearst until 1906.

The young reporter's first separate publication was a collection of songs entitled *Five Old English Ditties with Music by Carl Van Vechten*. These were "published for the author by N. Nelson, Chicago," in 1904. The songs belong to an intense period of musical inspiration in the autumn of 1904. The earliest, a setting of William Congreve's "Pious Selinda," has been dated by the composer October 19, 1904. The next was "A Lenten Ditty," dated October 31; the third, Congreve's "Petition," November 2; the fourth, Congreve's "Sabrina Wakes," November 7; and John Lyly's "Apelle's [sic] Song," November 20. The sources of the words show Mr. Van Vechten's wide literary interests and reading. It was Lyly who was to provide him, through this lyric, with the name of the tantalizing heroine of *The Blind Bow-Boy*, Campaspe Lorillard.

The manuscript of the songs is displayed beside the printed music and reveals a provocative early title – "The Love Songs of a Philanderer." These are not the only musical manuscripts among the Van Vechten papers. There is a baker's dozen of others, of which none has been published.

The next move in Carl Van Vechten's eastward progress came in 1906. He was not one to be confined to the life of a reporter, and he felt there were more stimulating cities to live in than Chicago. In October he began his connection with the *New York Times* as assistant music critic. It was a simple transition for the author of *Five Old English Ditties*.

The big musical event of Mr. Van Vechten's first sea-son with the *Times* was the suppression of Richard Strauss's opera *Salomé* at the Metropolitan Opera House after the single performance on January 22, 1907. The suppression was the occasion of a pitched battle between the conserva-tives and the liberals, and the combat was reported in the pages of the city's dailies. No accounts were more tellingly set forth than those which Mr. Van Vechten contributed to the *Times*.

Not content to limit himself solely to unsigned col-umns in the *New York Times*, Carl Van Vechten began to find outlets for free-lance articles. The first of these to be published in New York and under his own name appeared in the *Broadway Magazine* for January 1907 and was ac-cepted by Theodore Dreiser, who was then the editor. En-titled "Salomé: The Most Sensational Opera of the Age," the article in efficient fashion made use of the writer's knowl-edge of "the proposed production" at the Metropolitan. Dreiser, recognizing the timeliness of the subject and the abilities of the author, used it as the lead article.

Mr. Van Vechten, however, did not achieve his success without hard work. Another paper, on Barnard College at Columbia University, discussed with Dreiser at length, was given back for rewriting and was even then refused.

An interesting example of Carl Van Vechten's free-lancing is the ghost-written "Story of My Operatic Career. By Luisa Tetrazzini." The article appeared in the *Cosmopol-itan Magazine* for June 1908. It is not the only piece of his writing which appeared pseudonymously.

The impulse which impelled Carl Van Vechten out of

Cedar Rapids to Chicago and New York carried him as far east as Paris, where he filled the post of correspondent for the *New York Times* from June 1908 to April 1909. He covered news of a heterogeneous variety. One of his scrapbooks displays stories on tuberculosis serum, French naval disasters, Geraldine Farrar, Dr. Henry Van Dyke, and the Autumn salon.

If Mr. Van Vechten had been temperamentally an expatriate, he might have remained in Paris or returned there in the great American migration following the First World War. The city of his heart was New York. Thither he returned in the spring of 1909, to resume his duties as assistant music critic and to do some general reporting for the *Times*.

Resettled in New York – permanently, as it proved to be – Carl Van Vechten continued to extend his interests and his knowledge. From the autumn of 1909 he contributed to a variety of magazines, especially the *New Music Review*, for which in 1910 and 1911 he regularly produced "Foreign Notes" and "Facts, Rumors, and Remarks." In addition, during the 1910–11 season he wrote for the Symphony Society of New York its fortnightly *Symphony Society Bulletin*. A specially bound-up set of these papers reveals the scope of his program notes and the experience with which he came forward as an authoritative champion of modern music.

In May 1913 Mr. Van Vechten left the *New York Times* for the post of drama editor of the *New York Press*, which he held until the end of May 1914. During this season he reviewed some 130 dramatic entertainments – an indication of the stamina of both the theatre and the critics in the years before the First World War. His scrapbook is open to the review of Percy MacKaye's *A Thousand Years Ago*, the story of the Chinese princess Turandot. The winning young actress who was soon to become Mrs. Carl Van Vechten played the part of Zelima, and the critic ended his notice with the comment: "And Fania Marinoff's grace and beautiful voice give an added and necessary touch to the picture."

Fania Marinoff – the thirteenth child of her parents – had been born in Odessa, Russia, and had been brought to the United States when she was only five. Her childhood was spent in Denver, Colorado, and from the age of seven she showed a talent for recitation. Her first appearance in a play was as a boy in *Cyrano de Bergerac* with a Denver stock company. After she came to New York, she appeared in many successes – *Janice Meredith, The Man on the Box, Within the Law, Consequences*. Later in the run of *A Thousand Years Ago* she took over the lead role of Turandot. Miss Marinoff and Mr. Van Vechten were married in October 1914.

Among the magazines in which several articles by Carl Van Vechten appeared in the spring and summer of 1914 was the *Trend*, a monthly. That autumn, probably with the October issue, he took over the editorship for three months. In the October number he expounded the catholicity of the magazine and its standards: "THE TREND will publish articles, stories and verse by ANYBODY on ANY subject. . . . There is, on the other hand, a determination on the part of the editors to exclude stupidity, banality, sentimentality, cant, clap-trap morality, Robert W. Chambersism, sensationalism for its own sake, and ineffectuality of any kind." Mr. Van Vechten signed the piece Atlas. This manifesto was also printed separately as an advertising brochure entitled "Why and What."

THE ESSAYIST

Music after the Great War

Since a great part of Mr. Van Vechten's work had been concerned with music, it was appropriate that G. Schirmer, the New York music publishing house, should bring out his first book, *Music after the Great War and Other Studies.* It was as a critic and essayist that he was to be known to the public for many years. The maiden collection consisted of seven essays, of which five had previously appeared in such magazines as the *Trend*, the *New Music Review*, and *Rogue*. The final essay, indeed, had been published as late as the October 1915 *Forum*, and *Music after the Great War* appeared on December 22 of the same year. A table of contents on a paper label affixed to the front cover presented an appealing bill of fare. The collection was happily dedicated to Fania – now Fania Marinoff Van Vechten.

In two of the essays in particular Mr. Van Vechten demonstrated his ability to perceive and to call attention to work of permanent worth among the novelties of the moment. He has been master of ceremonies for many a talent. The two essays in question, which had not previously been published, were "The Secret of the Russian Ballet," completed only in November, and "Igor Strawinsky: A New Composer." The Library's copy of the collection carries Mr. Van Vechten's autograph annotations, made after publication, which correct, illuminate, and expand passages in the printed text. His article on Strawinsky was apparently the first original and extended study of the Russian composer to be published in the United States.

The subjects of two of the essays sent the author felicitations – and additional information. A letter from Igor Strawinsky is dated February 4, 1916, and corrects Mr. Van Vechten's statements about the dates of composition of "The Firebird" and "Le Sacre du Printemps." Writing on May 4, 1916, Adolphe Appia, the stage designer, promises to send details of the evolution of his theories and his work.

Music and Bad Manners

With his second book, *Music and Bad Manners*, published on November 14, 1916, Mr. Van Vechten began his long and happy connection with the publishing house of Alfred A. Knopf. Alfred Knopf and his wife, Blanche, became his close friends. Only one of his books – really a pamphlet – has since appeared with another imprint.

The format of *Music and Bad Manners*, with the contents label on the front cover, is reminiscent of *Music after the Great War*, and is shown in the exhibition in dummy form. The binding did not please. A second binding, put into use in June 1919, was modeled on the binding of *The Merry-Go-Round* (1918), and is characteristic of the individuality and smartness for which the young publishing house was to become famous.

Only one of the seven essays – "Shall We Realize Wagner's Ideals?" – had previously been published in its entirety, in the *Musical Quarterly*. A part of "A New Principle in

Music" had appeared in the *Russian Review*. The volume was dedicated to Mr. Van Vechten's father.

One of the Library's copies of *Music and Bad Manners* contains Mr. Van Vechten's annotations and corrections. These are most copious for the essay called "Spain and Music," which he was later to rework for another collection, *The Music of Spain*. It is amusing to know that he wrote the blurb for the dust-jacket when the book was issued in the second binding. It is a modest statement containing only two descriptive adjectives – "entertaining and stimulating" – both eminently suitable.

The collection was favorably received by the press. "Excellent essays . . . ," declared the *American Library Association Booklist*, "popular and scholarly, and distinguished by clarity and humor." The *Dial* was sure "his views will meet the approval of many close students of modern music." The *New York Call* found him "fundamentally and whole-heartedly progressive." The paper on Spanish music was particularly liked.

Two letters are displayed with *Music and Bad Manners*. The review which H. L. Mencken, in the postscript to a letter of November 27, 1916, promised to write of the book delighted both author and publisher. A quotation from it can be found on the dust-jacket with Mr. Van Vechten's own blurb.

The other letter (postmarked February 23, 1917) is an early souvenir of Mr. Van Vechten's friendship with Gertrude Stein, to whom he had sent a copy of the book. Miss Stein's famous cyclical poem on the nature of the rose is embossed on her stationery.

Interpreters and Interpretations

The next collection of essays dealing with music and musicians was entitled *Interpreters and Interpretations* and was published by Alfred Knopf on October 8, 1917. Once again the magic number was seven – only this time there were seven essays on interpreters and seven more on general musical subjects. Of the papers on individual artists – Olive Fremstad, Geraldine Farrar, Mary Garden, Chaliapin, Marietta Mazarin, Nijinsky – all but one on Yvette Guilbert had appeared in the *Bellman* during 1917. Four of the more general essays had previously seen print in a variety of magazines in 1917. One of the unpublished pieces was the first article to appear in the United States on the eccentric French composer Erik Satie.

The binding selected for *Interpreters and Interpretations* was ornate and employed three colors. When the sheets were bound up, ten copies were left with uncut fore-edges, of which one is displayed. Again the blurb on the dust-jacket was the work of the author.

The collection was dedicated, with a clever reference to its title, "to the unforgettable interpreter of Ariel . . Zelima . . . Louka . . . . Wendla . . . . . My Wife."

In the exhibition are corrected typescripts for some of the essays that were published in *Interpreters and Interpretations*. By this time Mr. Van Vechten was composing exclusively at the typewriter. There can be seen, for instance, two tables of contents: one corresponds to the volume as printed and an earlier one lists not only more essays but, in the "Interpretations" section, a different selection of material from what was ultimately published.

An interesting example of Mr. Van Vechten's painstaking method of work is found in three typescripts of the essay on Erik Satie. In the earliest of these, dated November 6, 1916, several pages exist in two versions. There are two typescripts dated November 16, 1916. The earlier of these shows a rearrangement of material and a substantial rewriting of the preceding version; it is also corrected and contains copious additions. The third typescript, though mostly a fair copy of the second, differs to some extent, particularly in the rearrangement of material, from the published version.

Mr. Van Vechten's interest in the essays in *Interpreters and Interpretations* did not cease with publication. The copy displayed, like his copies of the earlier collections, is carefully annotated.

"The proportion between scholarship and thought is not maintained," pontificated the *New Republic* in reviewing the collection in November 1917. "In the present book there might be more of the latter commodity." Contrariwise, the *New York Call* praised the volume because it discussed "things and people musical from the human rather than the academic standpoint."

After the publication of the book Mr. Van Vechten received from two of the singers the notes shown in the exhibition. Writing on October 27 [1917], Olive Fremstad warned him, "Of course I was interested in all that you said, although I am sure we might have some arguments concerning it were I to see you." Yvette Guilbert, who is widely known to admirers of Toulouse-Lautrec, the artist, spoke out with Gallic directness: "J'aurais un si vif plaisir de

vous connaitre cher Monsieur ne pouvez vous me tele-
phoner afin de prendre rendezvous for a cup of tea. . . ?"

Interpreters

In the autumn of 1920 Alfred Knopf brought out *Interpreters*, which, as the title suggests, was the first section of *Interpreters and Interpretations*. Some of the corrections found
in Mr. Van Vechten's annotated copy of the parent volume
were incorporated into the 1920 edition. Sixteen illustrations for the various articles were included – the first publication had been unillustrated – and an "Epilogue" devoted
to the relationship of interpreters and critics was added. The
binding of the book was similar to that first used on *The
Merry-Go-Round*, 1918, and imitated in 1919 on *Music and
Bad Manners*. This time the dedication mentioned Fania
Marinoff by name and included another of her successful
roles, Columbine.

The dust-jacket of the 1920 reprinting announced that
the "Interpretations" would be published later. This project
was never carried out.

The Merry-Go-Round

Alfred Knopf had now established the happy custom of
producing an annual volume by Carl Van Vechten. On
September 30, 1918, appeared a fourth collection of essays,
The Merry-Go-Round. Only four of the sixteen pieces had
not already seen magazine publication, one, indeed, having
appeared as recently as September 21 in the *Bellman*. Though
the emphasis was on musical material, there were also half a
dozen articles on the theatre and one straight literary essay,

previously unpublished, on Edgar Saltus, a neglected American novelist. This article was an early example of the essay of rediscovery at which Mr. Van Vechten was to become so adept.

On *The Merry-Go-Round* was used for the first time the attractive binding of black boards with colored paper labels on the backstrip and front cover. The volume shown in the exhibition is in the form of a dummy and beside it is another copy bearing on the dust-jacket the blurb written by the author.

With *The Merry-Go-Round* the *New Republic* began to thaw a bit toward Mr. Van Vechten. "The trouble with his school, with the Menckens and the Nathans, is not that their taste is bad, but that it is all disintegrated. . . . Mr. Van Vechten, however, deserves some mitigation of these strictures. . . . What saves him in the end is the freshness and warmth of his appreciations."

The early typescripts of *The Merry-Go-Round* reveal some of the essays to exist in more than one version. There are three stages of the opening essay, which in the version dated September 3, 1915, has no title; in the second version, undated, is entitled "Why Not Do It Yourself," and in the third, also undated, "In Defense of Bad Taste." A quickly perceived difference between the drafts can be found in the wording of the amusing "credit cards" for interior decorators. The actual names of the Baron de Meyer, best known as a glamour photographer, and of Elsie de Wolfe, later Lady Mendl, were dropped. Though intended at one point for publication in *Rogue* (notice the notation on the second draft), it appeared in the *Bellman* for August 3, 1918.

From one of the typescripts on display – which like all the others in this exhibition was the author's own handiwork – the printers set type. The author's corrected galley proofs are also exhibited.

The Merry-Go-Round was dedicated to Mary Garden, the great actress of the operatic stage. Her telegram of thanks for the dedication is displayed.

One of the most entertaining essays in the collection was "An Interrupted Conversation," a discussion, under unconventional circumstances, of the novelist George Moore. In a letter of December 2 [1918] Moore thanked Mr. Van Vechten for *The Merry-Go-Round* and chid him for his use of French words – a habit which Mr. Van Vechten explained he had picked up from Moore's *Confessions of a Young Man*.

The outstanding musical and literary critic of the preceding generation was James Gibbons Huneker (1860–1921), who is frequently mentioned in Mr. Van Vechten's essays – in the essay on Edgar Saltus, for example. Writing to Mr. Van Vechten on December 7, 1918, to praise *The Merry-Go-Round*, Huneker dwelt particularly upon Saltus. He remarked that of all American writers George Moore read only Walt Whitman and Saltus and that Saltus himself read only Emerson.

The Music of Spain

The interest shown in the essay "Spain and Music" in the second book encouraged Alfred Knopf to republish it on November 15, 1918, in a volume entitled *The Music of*

Spain. The volume is dedicated to Blanche Knopf. The binding is appropriately Spanish in color scheme.

Mr. Van Vechten made only slight corrections in the body of the essay proper but added nearly fifty pages of "Notes on the Text," which were gathered from his annotations in the copy of *Music and Bad Manners* in this exhibition. By reprinting from *The Merry-Go-Round* a study of a Spanish musical review called "The Land of Joy" and adding an unpublished study of Bizet's *Carmen* he rounded out "the only book in English on Spanish music."

The persistent scholarly interest which Mr. Van Vechten took in Spanish music is further illustrated by his handwritten annotations on the "Notes on the Text," which were themselves annotations on the text of the first printing of the essay.

The Music of Spain was the first of Mr. Van Vechten's books to be brought out in England – on May 17, 1920, by Kegan Paul, Trench, Trubner & Company. A preface was supplied by Pedro Morales, a musician and an advocate of Spanish music, who "was responsible for the first Orchestral and Chamber Music Concerts of Spanish Music in England," in 1918 and 1919.

Mentioned in the volume as one of the authorities on things Spanish was Havelock Ellis. In a letter of January 5, 1919, the English sociologist praises Mr. Van Vechten's "unusually sound" judgment. He protests, however, against the "theory that gypsies have no dances of their own but adopt those of the country they live in. . . ."

In the Garret

At the end of 1919, on December 15, a sixth collection of Carl Van Vechten's essays, entitled *In the Garret*, was brought out by Alfred Knopf. Four of the fifteen essays had already appeared in magazines or newspapers; another was to be published by Mencken in the January 1920 issue of the *Smart Set*. The binding was the black boards with paper labels that had become standard for Mr. Van Vechten's books. The volume was dedicated to the novelist Joseph Hergesheimer and his wife.

Once again the blurb was written by the author who imagined himself as ascending to the garret and perusing the contents of an ancient truck – "old books ..., faded photographs, wood-cuts and engravings, dog-eared periodicals, packets of letters, scraps of tabby, cashmere, and taffeta dresses, and theatre programmes. . . . This is a book of pictures, portraits, and moods." There are papers on literature, on the theatre, on composers, on music, on personalities.

The press received *In the Garret* with acclaim. "His touch is light and artistic," the *Bookman* announced. "His culture is Hunekeresque. His scholarship is musicianly, sometimes jazzy." The august London *Times* unbent sufficiently to say: "It is when he surveys the American scene that we go all the way with Mr. Van Vechten."

The typescripts of the papers in the collection are shown in early drafts. The final drafts, according to Mr. Van Vechten's note, have disappeared. From the corrected table of contents it can be seen that three essays intended for inclusion were dropped: "The Rape of the Madonna della Stella,"

"The Nightingale and the Peahen," and "How Mr. George Moore Rescued a Lady from Embarrassment," of which the latter two appeared a dozen years later in *Sacred and Profane Memories*. The epitaph on Oscar Hammerstein was added.

As usual, Mr. Van Vechten used his own copy of *In the Garret* for making notes and corrections. These are particularly noticeable in the article on "The Negro Theatre," perhaps the first important piece he wrote on the Negro in art. The volume is also stuffed with newspaper clippings and theatre programs.

Three letters, inspired by the book, are shown in the exhibition. Dorothy Hergesheimer – Mrs. Joseph Hergesheimer – told Carl Van Vechten in a letter of her pleasure in the dedication of *In the Garret*. The opening essay in the volume was "Variations on a Theme by Havelock Ellis." Writing to thank Mr. Van Vechten, Ellis admitted "a special interest in the first paper." The last letter is an expression of satisfaction with the essay on the Negro theatre by James Weldon Johnson, author of *The Autobiography of an Ex-Coloured Man*.

The Tiger in the House

While preparing articles for publication in *In the Garret*, Carl Van Vechten had been working since the beginning of 1919 on a book about another of his great interests – cats. This study, entitled *The Tiger in the House*, was completed on March 4, 1920, and published on October 21. Unlike its predecessors, the collection of essays on cats was composed of previously unpublished material. One chapter only, "The Cat in Music," appeared more or less simultaneously in the *Musical Quarterly* for October 1920.

The cat had long been an absorbing topic to Mr. Van Vechten, and about his pet he had collected an extraordinary amount of lore. This information he arranged in thirteen chapters – each essentially independent – dealing with the cat and the occult, the law, the theatre, the cat in music, in art, in poetry.

The volume was generously illustrated and published in a handsome format, half brown buckram and blue boards with a gold medallion. It was dedicated to Edna Kenton, a friend from Chicago days, and to Feathers, a Persian puss.

The early typescript of *The Tiger in the House* discloses that the title "Everybody's Tiger" was also being considered for the book. The way in which typed pages have been cut up and reassembled indicates the amount of work that went into this stage of the text. Accompanying the text are many notes and an early version of the table of contents which reveals the changes in arrangement through which the material went.

A second draft of the typescript, from which type was set, contains a few corrections in ink made by Mr. Van Vechten at the last moment. The proofs exist in first proof, first revise, and final revise state, carefully corrected and rechecked by the author.

At the time the typescript of the book was delivered to Mr. Knopf, Carl Van Vechten wrote his publisher an illuminating letter on the purpose, the structure, and the method of the book.

The first six chapters epitomize the history and the character of the cat. The history is inserted subtly, like castor oil in a sweet drink. The chapters on the Occult and Folklore are really part of Chapter II, Treating of Traits, but are too long and too important not to be treated separately. The general knowledge thus diffused in these first six chapters is really essential to the reader who wishes to follow intelligently the last chapters, which are devoted to the uses of the cat in art. Of course an absolute cut and dried following of this scheme would mean a dry book, and so I have mixed them up somewhat. . . .

The first edition of *The Tiger in the House* was limited to 2000 copies; each copy was luxuriously boxed. The box-top was ornamented with a blurb written by the author and decorated with a cut of a cat – "Minette Washes" by Gottfried Mind. Upon the objections of a Philadelphia bookseller, the second edition of the book, which was ready on July 19, 1924, was provided with a cut of a cat with a muff by Grandville, to which no exception could be taken.

The text of the second edition was corrected by Mr. Van Vechten from the annotated copy of the first edition shown in the exhibition. In fact, the printers seem to have worked directly from this very copy.

The Tiger in the House was the second of Mr. Van Vechten's books to be published in England. This time American sheets were used and still another cut of a cat was placed on the dust wrapper.

The volume has had a lasting sale. It was reprinted in this country in 1936 with an introduction by Mr. Van

Vechten and in England in 1938. From the English edition the introduction was inadvertently omitted.

Edna Kenton, herself a writer of experience as a novelist and a biographer, expressed in a letter her enthusiasm at having the book dedicated to her. Arthur Davison Ficke, the poet and student of Japanese art, who lent many of the illustrations for the book, wrote a poem of welcome on a note from Mr. Van Vechten offering him a copy of the book. Ficke's poem begins:

> Oh let the Tiger growl within mine house!
> I'll treat her gently as a suckling mouse
> Or young Celestial Dragon or Bright Bird
> Whose madrigals in Xanadu are heard.

The Tiger was well received in the press as well as in the house. "The book is a revelation," declared the *Bookman*, "concerning the more or less important part which cats have played in history and literature." The *Boston Evening Transcript* was taken with "the suggestive ingenuity of the title" and "the far-reaching skill with which he has amassed and arranged his facts [in a way] that blends both fact and imagination."

Lords of the Housetops

The next year—on July 28, 1921—Alfred Knopf brought out an anthology of thirteen tales about cats entitled *Lords of the Housetops*. One of these, Balzac's "Afflictions of an English Cat," Carl Van Vechten had himself translated, and he provided a general preface, which had been written on April 6, 1920, in the flush of enthusiasm that followed the publication of *The Tiger in the House*.

The *New York Times* liked the "clever title" of the anthology. The *New York Post* praised the preface as brief and vivacious and acclaimed Mr. Van Vechten as "our most eminent authority on cats." The collection of tales was sufficiently popular for Mr. Knopf to republish it in 1930 in the Borzoi Pocket Books series.

"Feathers"

A final tribute to cats by Carl Van Vechten, indeed a postscript to *The Tiger in the House,* was published in 1931 by Random House as one of its *Prose Quartos.* Entitled "Feathers," it was an elegy on the Persian cat that had appeared in the final pages of *The Tiger* and had shared the dedication with Edna Kenton. The tone of love, of guilt, of regret, is perfectly conveyed.

Appreciation of the quality of "Feathers" was expressed by two friends of Mr. Van Vechten's, ladies of reputation as writers of fiction. Ellen Glasgow, a devoted lover of animals, called it "a gem of an essay." Ettie Stettheimer, who wrote under the pseudonym of Henrie Waste, found it "so charmingly written and so happily, it purrs." With keen-edged wit she added that until she read of the circumstances of Feathers' death she had thought she "belonged to the only class of creatures (pt. of view of sex) not found in the animal world – voluntary spinsters – (to dress it in the present Victorian style). . . ."

Red

Ten years after his first collection of musical essays appeared, Mr. Van Vechten brought out his last. In the interval he had discovered an outstanding ability to write fiction and had become absorbed in a new set of problems and satisfactions. He had reversed the usual process: the successful critic had become the successful novelist. It also pleased his sense of the dramatic that he should leave the old field of music and the drama soon after his fortieth birthday. For nearly twenty years he had "attended an opera or a play nearly every evening, and, for long stretches, nearly every afternoon as well." He had long held "the firm belief that after forty the cells hardened and that prejudices were formed which precluded the possibility of the welcoming of novelty."

His point of view is clearly set forth in "A Valedictory," which serves as an introduction to *Red: Papers on Musical Subjects*, which Alfred Knopf published on January 19, 1925. Twenty-five copies were bound up uncut, one of which is shown here, and this made them a quarter inch taller than the regular edition. The binding, though stylishly plain, was not like that of earlier volumes of essays but like that of the most recent Van Vechten novel. The collection was dedicated to the versatile artist Ralph Barton, well-known for his illustrations for *Gentlemen Prefer Blondes*.

Ralph Barton's genuine pleasure at the dedication of *Red* communicates itself from his letter of May 8, 1924: "I shall promise you to try to live up to it. It will be a turning point in my life. For example, since it is a book of musical essays, I'll begin by buying season tickets to all the orchestras and by engaging a box at the opera."

In the early 1920s Carl Van Vechten formed the entertaining habit of having his signature on his contracts with Alfred Knopf witnessed by someone in his circle who was also much in the public eye. It was doubtless the appropriateness of his nickname that prompted Mr. Van Vechten on June 9, 1924, to ask Red Lewis to witness the contract for *Red: Papers on Musical Subjects*. The witness used his official signature – Sinclair Lewis. (All the contracts in the exhibition were lent through the kindness of Mr. Alfred A. Knopf.)

For *Red* Mr. Van Vechten selected from his earlier books "such papers on musical subjects as I care to preserve, save for a few dealing with specific composers, later to find their niches in a book to be entitled Excavations, which will also include papers on certain figures in the literary world. . . ." There was nothing in *Red* from *Music after the Great War*, but there was one essay from *Music and Bad Manners*; three from *Interpreters and Interpretations* and three from *In the Garret*; two from *The Merry-Go-Round*; and three that had been published only in periodicals. The blurb was once again the work of the author, who carefully pointed out that the earlier volumes of essays were out of print.

The *Saturday Review of Literature* found the collection "entertaining, witty, clever. . . ." The "vivacity" of the writing and "the myriad shafts of suggestion it throws off" were praised by the *New York Tribune*. The *Independent*, which had been upset by Mr. Van Vechten's "sophisticated, rather improper fiction," was delighted with the "culture . . . genuine and broad" of *Red*.

Even though the essays in the collection were being reprinted for the second, third, or even fourth time, Mr. Van Vechten retyped and corrected them all, as the typescript shown in the exhibition reveals. It was characteristic of his unceasing interest in and care for his text. Type was set from this typescript.

Excavations

A companion volume to *Red* was *Excavations: A Book of Advocacies*, published on January 13, 1926. It contained sixteen essays all of which had previously seen print: one in *Interpreters and Interpretations*; one in *The Merry-Go-Round*; four in *In the Garret*; four as introductions to books by others; six in periodicals only. There were four on "specific composers" – Delibes, Sullivan, Albeniz, Satie – as promised in *Red*. The study of Ronald Firbank, put together from several sources, was the first on the English novelist to be published in the United States.

To take care of collectors' interests Alfred Knopf bound up a few uncut copies, with a paper label and no design in blind on the front cover or borzoi on the back. These copies are a quarter-inch taller than the trade edition.

It was H. L. Mencken who on April 16, 1925, witnessed the signing of the contract.

The text of *Excavations*, like that of *Red*, was retyped by Mr. Van Vechten and thoroughly gone over. With the corrected typescript, which was used by the printers, are shown the corrected galley and page proofs.

It must have been gratifying to Mr. Van Vechten to receive letters of appreciation from some of the subjects of his excavations. "I feel excavated indeed . . . ," wrote Henry Blake Fuller. "Don't use the word 'apologies' – you who have done for me what scarcely anyone else has even thought to do." With some pathos, Arthur Machen declared "I was saying to my wife, after reading some of it: 'The fact is, Van Vechten likes reading things that other people won't read; that's why he likes reading me'. . . . Things are not going very well with me now. Knopf has put me before the American public to the best possible advantage; & you & other kindly critics have done your utmost: but the public in your country as in mine, though taken to the writer, will not drink!" From beside the pyramids Ronald Firbank wrote, "A thousand salaams for 'Excavations' just come. I shall read it with delight – not least the chapter on Ronald."

And Ralph Van Vechten, to whom it was dedicated, was pleased at "the first honor I have ever received of this kind."

As usual Mr. Van Vechten supplied the copy for the dust-jacket. Once more he was careful to point out that the earlier volumes of essays were "out of print and will not be republished."

The critics received the collection well. The *New York Herald Tribune* found the essays "still interesting and entertaining now that they are reprinted." "The worst that can be said of him," thought the London *Saturday Review*, "is that, while he never fails to interest, he does not convince." The paper on Oscar Hammerstein was praised on both sides of the Atlantic: "Valuable as biography," declared the *Nation*, "and moving as characterization."

Sacred and Profane Memories

Though Mr. Van Vechten may have thought he would bring out no more volumes of essays, his last published book was just such a collection, entitled *Sacred and Profane Memories*. For it he gathered together pieces previously published in an earlier collection now out of print, like "La Tigresse" and "The Folksongs of Iowa" from *In the Garret*; or pieces that had appeared only in magazines, like "The Tin Trunk" and "An Old Daguerreotype" from the Richmond, Virginia, *Reviewer*, to which he had so often contributed. There was also an hitherto unpublished account of the outbreak of World War I, entitled "July-August 1914." There were altogether twelve pieces, exclusive of a foreword and a bibliography. The volume was dedicated to his friends Florine Stettheimer the painter, Carrie Stettheimer her sister, and the novelist Henrie Waste, known privately as Ettie Stettheimer.

The collection was published by Alfred Knopf on April 15, 1932, in an edition of 2000 numbered copies. Mr. Van Vechten had asked to have the book appear as nearly as possible on the day that his first novel, *Peter Whiffle*, had made its bow a decade before. The dust-jacket of the volume of essays was designed by Prentiss Taylor. Cassell and Company of London issued the American sheets under their title-page.

The contract for Mr. Van Vechten's last book was signed as witness by Eugene O'Neill on November 20, 1931.

Though Carl Van Vechten had already prepared the essays in *Sacred and Profane Memories* for publication with the greatest care, he characteristically took pains over their publication. Each essay was revised and retyped, as the typescripts shown in the exhibition testify. There are also numerous ink corrections. Mr. Van Vechten was ever the self-exacting artist. Type was set from these typescripts. The galleys show the usual final polishing.

The Stettheimer sisters sent Carl Van Vechten a telegram wishing "a long and happy life to our godchild." Other friends of long standing described the pleasure which *Sacred and Profane Memories* had given them. James Branch Cabell wrote, "It is not extraordinary of course that you should get more of yourself into these casual essays than into a novel, and I like vastly the intimate and companionable result." With the eye of a fellow craftsman Mr. Cabell compared the early with the final published versions of some of the essays and meted out praise and reproof. An English friend, Matthew Phipps Shiel, author of many fantastic novels, wrote Mr. Van Vechten, "One sees in it a fresh fellow who has the merit of being himself, and not another man. And shrewd in the corner of one eye."

Sacred and Profane Memories appeared in the worst year of the Depression, and memories of happy days were not much to the taste of that sober time. The *New York Herald Tribune* thought them "neither sufficiently sacred nor yet sufficiently profane." The *New Republic*, more socially conscious than ever, found the collection "quaint," the work of "a pre-war dilettante." The *Saturday Review of Literature*, however, praised the "delicacy and charm" of the volume.

THE NOVELIST

Peter Whiffle

In the spring of 1922 Carl Van Vechten presented to the public another facet of his abilities. His first novel, *Peter Whiffle: His Life and Works*, appeared on April 14, a bright bolt from the blue. According to his own account in *Red*, he had taken a first step toward fiction around 1918. There is, for instance, a reference to one Peter Whiffle in "La Tigresse" in *In the Garret*, published in 1919. Mr. Van Vechten frankly admitted that he attempted fiction because there was some chance of profit to be hoped from it, whereas most of his volumes of criticism had been remaindered. He also felt that if one is able to write it at all, fiction is easier to write than criticism.

Five years before the publication of the novel, the character of Peter Whiffle began to take shape in Carl Van Vechten's imagination. Peter was to be presented to the world under the name of Sasha in a short story called "Undecided Sasha," of which three typescripts exist. The first version – built around the abortive trip to Bermuda found in the novel – is dated January 9, 1917, and is heavily corrected in pencil. The hero is named Sasha Idonsky. In the second version, which is undated, very slightly corrected in ink, and stops after the fourth page, he is Sasha Broadwood. The third version, undated and corrected at the typewriter, breaks off in the middle of a sentence in the middle of the fifth page.

The first typescript of *Peter Whiffle* begins with an appropriate note: "(this idea came to me on March 28, 1919 in the New York Public Library . . .)." Though corrected, it bears relatively few corrections for the first draft of a first novel. The second draft, which is placed beside it, is more liberally corrected. The final draft, from which type was set, bears a few last-minute changes. It is dated April 29, 1921.

The galleys show how Mr. Van Vechten kept polishing his style to the last moment. There is hardly a galley that does not carry the mark of his correcting pen.

The first of the contracts on which Mr. Van Vechten's signature was witnessed by a celebrity was that for *Peter Whiffle*. The signing of the contract for his first novel, on November 22, 1921, was happily witnessed by Fania Marinoff.

The first issue of *Peter Whiffle*, bound in orange boards, was especially produced by Alfred Knopf for the bookseller friends of Borzoi Books in an edition of 50 copies. A leaf bearing the limitation note is pasted between the half-title and title-page. The trade issue was bound in batik boards and without the limitation leaf. The novel was dedicated "To the Memory of My Mother, Ada Amanda Fitch Van Vechten."

The blurb on the dust-jacket was the work of the author, and he makes it plain that *Peter Whiffle* contains characters drawn – at least in part – from living originals. The most obvious characterization was undoubtedly that of Mabel Ganson Evans Dodge Sterne Luhan as Edith Dale of the novel.

The press greeted *Peter Whiffle* enthusiastically. True, the *New York Evening Post* held against the novel one of its most attractive qualities: "Perhaps good nature is what is wrong. . . . Certainly it needs something acid, some flavor of bitterness to sharpen its mild tang." The tang of the book was what was right on most palates. " 'Peter Whiffle' is sparkling stuff," thought the *New York Times*. "It is delightful fare after the solid dishes of our solemn realists." Carl Van Doren gave Mr. Van Vechten high praise in the *Nation*: "He knows how to laugh, he scorns solemnity, he has filled his book with wit and erudition. He is a civilized writer."

Mabel Dodge Luhan, the Edith Dale of the novel, wrote in May 1922 from Taos, New Mexico, with feminine curiosity about the success of *Peter Whiffle*. Toward the end of October she wrote again, mentioning "a very amusing evening" when D. H. Lawrence read aloud from the novel. Gertrude Stein, another figure in the story, expressed her satisfaction with the way she had been put in it: "There is one certainty one could never be more pleasantly more faithfully nor more gently in it than when one is put in it by you."

Another friend sent a copy of a letter Mr. Van Vechten had written his father about the meaning of *Peter Whiffle*. The elder Mr. Van Vechten had circulated copies like the one shown in the exhibition among his friends all over the country.

When the novel had gone through twelve printings, Alfred Knopf brought out in September 1927 an edition illustrated with photographs of places and persons appearing in the novel. It was bound in pictorial boards – an issue covered in silk limited to 20 copies; an unlimited issue in paper – showing Ralph Barton's map of Paris.

There is also displayed the first English edition, published by Grant Richards, with a quotation from Hugh Walpole on the dust-jacket. Beside it is the first Modern Library edition, which appeared in 1929.

The Blind Bow-Boy

In *Peter Whiffle* Carl Van Vechten had presented a picture of Bohemian New York in the relatively quiet days before the First World War. In his second novel, *The Blind Bow-Boy*, he introduced his readers to the more worldly, fashionable, and feverish life of the city in the early 1920s. The story is constructed around the *education sentimentale* of the hero. The attendant nymph of the god Eros is Campaspe Lorillard, the ideal sophisticate of her time.

The novel, which was dedicated to Alfred A. Knopf, "my publisher and my friend," appeared on August 15, 1923. The decorative boards of the first trade edition (3500 copies) were from a design by the English artist Lovat Fraser. There was also a large-paper edition, limited to 115 copies, in green paper boards. Freak copies of the trade edition – issued for the use of salesmen before the frontispiece was ready and lacking the green rules on the title-page – are known to exist.

In its first draft, which was completed on June 8, 1922, Mr. Van Vechten's second novel was called *Daniel Matthews' Tutor*. The name of the hero, Daniel Matthews, was corrected by hand in the typescript to Harold Prewett. The first typescript runs to 147 heavily corrected pages and ends with attention focused on Campaspe Lorillard.

The second typescript, which is dated August 6, 1922, carries the final title, *The Blind Bow-Boy*. The text has now been expanded by one third; there are 195 typed pages. The ironic touch with which the novel closes has been added in longhand: the reader's attention is lifted from Campaspe Lorillard and brought to rest on Harold Prewett, with whom the story opened.

The third and final typescript, which is dated October 28, 1922, bears many pen and ink alterations. From it type was set: it carries the compositors' marks. The process of polishing was, indeed, continued through various stages of proof, of which galleys are shown.

The signing of the contract for *The Blind Bow-Boy*, which occurred on November 10, 1922, was witnessed by Hugh Walpole. The novel was to remain the Englishman's favorite. The signature of the publisher gives this contract the added distinction of bearing the signature of the dedicatee.

Mr. Van Vechten used an especially bound up set of sheets to make corrections for later printings of *The Blind Bow-Boy*; on the half-title he has listed them – for the second, third, fourth, and fifth. Within a year the novel ran into six printings.

Grant Richards brought out the English edition in October 1923, and on the title-page of the copy shown here he wrote, "To Carl Van Vechten who appears to me today to be one of the most amiable of authors and whose books I am proud to publish." The English publisher found it advisable to delete from his edition four or five passages, like the comments on the Duke of Middlebottom and his notepaper.

The blurb on the dust-jacket was the work of the author, who "has sworn before a notary public that his only purpose in creating The BLIND BOW-BOY was to amuse." Mr. Van Vechten anonymously explained: "This book is not 'romantic' or 'realistic' or 'life' or 'art' . . . and no ideas are concealed beneath its surface."

Reviewing the novel in the *New York World*, Heywood Broun denied the author's avowals: "Despite Mr. Van Vechten's protestations, this is very clearly an uplift story. He propagandizes for all those brave beings who seek, in spite of tyranny, to follow their own inclinations." Ernest Boyd declared in the *Nation*, "One turns from 'The Blind Bow-Boy' with as definite an impression of New York in 1922 as one gets of Paris under the Second Empire from [Zola]." In the *Dial* Edmund Wilson made flattering comparisons with Max Beerbohm and Anatole France.

Of course there were critics who disapproved of the impression of New York and the morality. "A perverse, readable, and amusing story," cried the *Bookman*, "which is as unworthy of him as it is nasty." The great London *Times* remonstrated that "his book has the air of great vitality and zest however frivolously misapplied."

Joseph Hergesheimer, who was himself a careful craftsman, wrote Mr. Van Vechten on September 25, 1923, to commend *The Blind Bow-Boy* for "the wholly formal correctness of the structure" and "the amazing, the sterile, the satirical conclusion. This is a better book for these reasons, dear Carl, than Peter." Writing from France on September 27, Sinclair Lewis hailed the novel as "superb . . . impertinent, subversive, resolutely and completely wicked. . . . You prove that New York is as sophisticated as any foreign capital. . . ." With characteristic wit and vigor H. L. Mencken praised *The Blind Bow-Boy* in a letter of August 22, 1923, as "an excellent piece of work." "I am two-thirds through the book," he added by way of testimonial, "and find my hay-fever much improved."

The novel was not only widely read; it also had its effect upon one of the more exotic artists of the period, Hans Henning von Voigt, who worked under the name of Alastair. In a style that obviously derived from Aubrey Beardsley, Alastair gave his interpretation of the characters in Mr. Van Vechten's novel. The drawing of Campaspe, shown in the exhibition, conveys more of the atmosphere of the 1890s than of the 1920s.

The Tattooed Countess

The Tattooed Countess, Carl Van Vechten's third novel, appeared on August 15, 1924, exactly a year to the day after *The Blind Bow-Boy*. The size of the first printing was more than double that of the preceding book. There were 160 large paper copies and 7500 trade copies. Mr. Knopf had opened his own London office, and the English edition of *The Tattooed Countess*, which appeared in 1926, bears his imprint. A French version, *La Comtesse Tatouée* – "dans l'Amérique de 1900, une comtesse et son chérubin gigolo" – was published in 1932, by Éditions de la Madeleine.

The novel was dedicated to Hugh Walpole and, by the way of compliment, refers in passing to some of Walpole's characters – the Duchess of Wrexe, for instance – as if they were friends of the Countess's.

The contract was signed on June 3, 1924, in the presence of Theodore Dreiser. It was Dreiser who had accepted the first article by Mr. Van Vechten to appear in a New York magazine.

Before starting to write *The Tattooed Countess* Carl Van Vechten made pages of notes. Some are concerned with the characters and the events of their lives. Others are guides to the clothes, slang, songs, reading, theatre, and celebrities of the time – the local and temporal color of the novel.

The first draft was begun on March 26, 1923, and completed on June 5. The title was fixed, but the original subtitle reads: "Scenes of American provincial life in 1897." The subject is not merely an episode in the middle life of the Countess Nattatorrini but a chapter in the cultural history of Maple Valley, Iowa, to which the former Ella Poore returns on a visit to her sister. It is to be noted that the novel opens on June 17, 1897, which was Carl Van Vechten's seventeenth birthday. At first the heroine had been called Countess Appassionata and her past was romanticized. The first typescript was, of course, worked over in longhand.

In the second draft, which was begun on June 20 and completed on August 2, 1923, there is much rewriting. The Countess is given a more convincing, if more sordid, past experience: the lover who has just grown tired of her is not a dashing aristocrat of twenty-two named Maurice but a handsome, commonplace opera singer of twenty-two, Toni, who is interested only in her money. The character of his successor, Gareth Johns of Maple Valley, is much developed. Johns makes his first appearance in *The Tattooed Countess*, and many resemblances between him and his creator might be traced. On the other hand, Clara Barnes, who had already appeared in *Peter Whiffle* as a student of voice in Paris, is here a very young girl who loses Gareth to the Countess.

The third typescript is dated October 20, 1923. For the first time the final and satirical subtitle appears, "a romantic novel with a happy ending." Though type was set from this draft, it bears the usual polishing in longhand.

The process of sharpening the style continued through the proof. Galley and page proofs show unnecessary adjectives deleted, adjectives added to clarify a picture, an overworked adjective – "brilliant sun" – replaced by one that was fresher – "lambent sun."

Among the preliminary pages of *The Tattooed Countess* was published the first bibliography of Mr. Van Vechten's work. Corrected proof indicates how careful the author was to keep even this abbreviated list accurate.

The pictorial dust-wrapper for *The Tattooed Countess* was the work of Mr. Van Vechten's friend Ralph Barton and the blurb that of Alfred Knopf. The publisher did not overstate the worth of the new novel. With it Carl Van Vechten demonstrated that he was able to write fiction which evoked more than a smart and entertaining atmosphere. *Peter Whiffle* had emphasized the fantastic; *The Blind Bow-Boy*, the sophisticated. Underneath its bland and amused surface *The Tattooed Countess* was a novel of character, of situation, of manners.

The reviewers were pleased with the book, although they seem not to have thoroughly understood it. In the *Nation* Joseph Wood Krutch, who denied the characters the gift of life, found the novel marked by "grace of style and . . . wit." The comic spirit was recognized by all. "Thoroughly readable," declared the *Literary Review*. "Easy reading, entertaining and light," pronounced the *New York Times*.

Though the professional reviewers overlooked many of the subtleties of *The Tattooed Countess*, Mr. Van Vechten's friends were more discerning. Among them were some of the best-known writers of the day on both sides of the Atlantic, and the differences in their interpretation and evaluation testify to the vitality of the study. Hugh Walpole, to whom the novel was dedicated, wrote the author about the Countess: "On her own bottom, so to speak, she's not I think so good as my beloved 'Bow Boy' – But I think she's infinitely more interesting and promising. . . . It shows how true an artist you are that you should step out and develop new talents."

Somerset Maugham, on the contrary, felt that the new novel was on a higher level of creation than *The Blind Bow-Boy*. "Not one in a hundred of your readers will ever see how witty and brilliant and entrancing it is," he wrote Mr. Van Vechten in a letter that was in part quoted on the dust-jacket of the English edition. He admired "the discretion with which you have let your exquisite humor get its own laughter," and cited the relationship of the young hero with the Countess as an example of unforced irony.

When he was sent the novel and asked to design the dust-jacket, Ralph Barton declared it to be "at least twice as good" as its predecessor and mentioned the enthusiasm of his wife, Carlotta, later Mrs. Eugene O'Neill. Barton drew many parallels between his own and Mr. Van Vechten's experience as boys in the Middle West. Alastair, who had done the extra drawings for *The Blind Bow-Boy*, wrote a soul-sick letter which suggests that he might do a set of illustrations for *The Tattooed Countess*.

Other writers who left their mark on the fiction of this century expressed their excitement over the new novel. From St. Raphael, F. Scott Fitzgerald wrote Mr. Van Vechten that "the resumé of her past & the 1st 'sketches' of Iowa as you call them (the Parcae, the Reception) ect. [sic] are unbeatable." James Branch Cabell praised the "development of Gareth from the fourteenth chapter onward." Another Virginia novelist, Ellen Glasgow, confessed, "I dont seem to be able to shake the democratic dust of Maple Valley from my clothes. You have made it wonderfully vivid, and how I should have hated it if I had been your temperamental heroine! Poor creature! For I see quite clearly that it came to the Seine at last, and that the Freudian minded youth she eloped with ascended to places higher and more material than Mr. Cabells."

In 1925 Paramount Pictures, without help from the author, produced *A Woman of the World* "from a novel by Carl Van Vechten." The unnamed and almost unrecognizable novel was *The Tattooed Countess*. The Countess was

played by Pola Negri, and Gareth Johns by Charles Em-
mett Mack. But Gareth's place in the Countess' life was
handed over to a new character, Richard Granger, the District Attorney of Maple Valley, Iowa, played by Holmes
Herbert.

The original story was naturally distasteful to Hollywood and the movie-going public. Henry Blake Fuller sent
Mr. Van Vechten the advance publicity which was issued
in Chicago for the picture: " 'A Woman of the World' is
a young woman of the world, not a wasted worldling
avidly clutching at youth in the form of a village boy. Now
her grand passion is for the adult district attorney of Maple
Valley, Ia. And the Countess Nattatorrini marries him and
they live happily ever after. But not before she has lashed
him with a blacksnake and taught him to fetch cigarettes."
Resemblances to *The Tattooed Countess* had been painstakingly obliterated and apologized for.

The film was released in December 1925. Mr. Van
Vechten found the picture "one of the worst Ive ever seen.
. . . I saw it exactly once at a preview for my benefit. . . ."
He added, "Fortunately, they changed the story completely
and even the title: so I didnt have to blush when I passed a
picture palace where it was showing."

Firecrackers

The mood of Mr. Van Vechten's fourth novel, *Firecrackers*,
is totally different from that of *The Tattooed Countess*. It is
a curious blend of the tone of *Peter Whiffle* and *The Blind
Bow-Boy*. The new story is a fantasy on the paradoxical

nature of love. The symbols employed belong to New York in the mid-1920s, indeed, the story takes place two years after the close of *The Blind Bow-Boy* and in the same environment. That novel also provides the principal characters – Campaspe Lorillard, Paul Moody, and Gunnar O'Grady, brother of Zimbule O'Grady. There also flash through *Firecrackers* characters from other novels – Edith Dale from *Peter Whiffle*; Gareth Johns and Ella Nattatorrini from *The Tattooed Countess*.

Firecrackers was published by Alfred Knopf in August 1925 in an edition of 205 large-paper copies and a regular trade issue of 10,000 copies. The large-paper copies were bound in decorative boards; the trade issue in yellow cloth with a design in red around the edges. Two years later it appeared in England with the Knopf London imprint.

The novel is dedicated to James Branch Cabell. On the contract, which was signed on November 30, 1924, Cabell's signature appears as witness. This contract was the third with Alfred Knopf signed in 1924.

The first draft of *Firecrackers* was completed more than a year before publication. The writing progressed quickly. The first typescript, which carries no title, is dated: "commenced June 7, 1924 at 3 p.m." and "finished July 23, 1924." There exist a few typed notes made in preparation, mostly for dialogue and for descriptive touches. The typescript shows some corrections in ink: notably the name of the *enfant terrible*, Berenice, is altered to Consuelo. Significantly the novel ends with the athlete Gunnar O'Grady's falling to his death from the high wire.

In the second typescript the final title and subtitle have

been given the story: "Firecrackers a realistic novel." The first page reads, "(second draught commenced August 2, at 12.50 p.m.)." The typescript was completed on September 10, 1924. The second version is much more extensively corrected than the first. The ending has been entirely reworked: Gunnar does not fall from the high wire but cauterizes his heart with liquor and sex. The scene was almost in its final form. The last sentence, however, had not yet been evolved. In the second draft it reads:

What do you mean? Is he dead?

No, not dead, Paul replied, not dead. He's just beginning to turn over a new leaf.

From the third typescript, which is dated October 26, 1924, type was set. Yet it contains copious ink corrections, indications of the final polishing. The last sentence has now been charged with implication:

What do you mean? Has he killed himself? . . .

I don't know, he replied.

Mr. Van Vechten continued to point up the prose style as he received galley and page proofs. The final page of the page proof is shown to illustrate the sharpening process.

The varying reactions to *Firecrackers* of Mr. Van Vechten's friends testify to the appeal of the story. To James Branch Cabell, who was "wholly proud to be the dedicatee," it was "far and away above your preceding best." F. Scott Fitzgerald placed it on a par with *The Blind Bow-Boy* and above the other two novels: "It seems to me that this rather than *The Tatoed* [sic] *Countess* is your true line of genius. . . . I wish you could personally create a new form for that sort of novel, something lying between the

almost unbearable sequence of humor in Sulieka [Max
Beerbohm's *Zuleika Dobson*] and the almost equally an-
noying diffuseness of South Wind. You in *The Blind Bow-
Boy* have come nearer to doing it so far than either Huxley
or Firbank." Louis Bromfield, on the contrary, enjoyed
Firecrackers most for the reappearance of characters from
The Tattooed Countess.

Elinor Wylie, a novelist as well as a poet, expressed an
opinion shared by others with less sensitivity than herself.
"Long before Carl Van Doren called it austere," she wrote
to Mr. Van Vechten, "I called it tragic. It really is almost
unbearably tragic; I expected the wit & the glitter, but not
the dark other side of the coin."

The unconventional blurb on the dust-jacket of *Firecrackers* is again the work of the author, who amused himself by citing the reproaches made by critics about his earlier work: "Another of Carl Van Vechten's unimportant,
light novels, disfigured by all this author's customary annoying mannerisms: choice of a meaningless title, rejection
of quotation marks, adoption of obsolete or unfamiliar
words, an obstinate penchant for cataloguing, and an apparent refusal to assume a reverent attitude towards the
ideals of life which are generally held most precious."

Mr. Van Vechten must have been delighted by the way
his own strictures anticipated some of the critics. " 'Firecrackers' is one of those obscure performances which leave
the beholder puzzled . . .," declared the *Nation*. "As usual,
the style is witty, cynical and hard," the *New York Times*
warned, "perhaps a little harder than in the other novels.
Mr. Van Vechten's mannerisms are more pronounced, the

odd word and the cataloguing sometimes annoying." Albert Payson Terhune dismissed the novel in the *New York Evening Post* as "inconsequential decadent mirth cut off the same sleazily shimmery pattern as Aldous Huxley's *Antic Hay*."

Other critics were more perspicacious. Henry Blake Fuller in the *Saturday Review of Literature* praised the way Mr. Van Vechten's "extremely individualistic pages lead one on . . . irresistibly." In the *New York Tribune* Carl Van Doren declared, "He has hit upon a world in which his imagination moves easily. He has invented a language which is his and no one else's. . . . Within the limits of his interests, which means also his capacities, almost anything may be henceforth expected of him."

Nigger Heaven

Carl Van Vechten's interest in the Negro's contribution to the intellectual life of the United States was deep and long-standing. He followed and acclaimed the work of the Negro in literature, music, and the theatre. He formed close friendships with Negro writers, singers, and actors; he was at home in their homes and they in his. He contributed introductions to their books and wrote articles about their work. He was their friend and their champion.

Mr. Van Vechten's knowledge and understanding of the Negro found its best-known expression in his fifth novel, *Nigger Heaven*. For years he had been familiar with Harlem and had realized its place not only in the life of contemporary New York but also in that of the whole country. He recognized the dramatic material waiting there for the novelist, who up to now had disregarded it.

Nigger Heaven, the third volume dedicated to Fania Marinoff, appeared on August 20, 1926. In addition to the first printing of 16,000 copies in brown cloth with blue stamping, the trade edition, there was a large-paper edition in flowered cloth limited to 205 copies. It was the biggest first printing that any of Mr. Van Vechten's books had had up to this time, though with each successive volume the size of the first printing had been increased. By the end of December *Nigger Heaven* had gone into nine printings. The English edition, published in October 1926, carried the London imprint of Alfred Knopf.

On March 18, 1926, James Weldon Johnson witnessed the contract. Mr. Johnson was to be a staunch defender of the novel from its detractors.

As usual, there exist three typescripts of *Nigger Heaven* painstakingly corrected in ink. The labor which Carl Van Vechten expended upon his prose is nowhere more graphically illustrated than in the first paragraph of the novel. The three versions of this paragraph show the evolution of the description of Anatole Longfellow, alias the Scarlet Creeper, toward ever increasing vividness.

In the first typescript, which was started on November 3 and completed on December 22, 1925, the portrait is sketched:

> Anatole Longfellow, alias the Scarlet Creeper, sidled aimfully down the East side of Seventh Avenue. He was dressed in a tight fitting sheapherd's [sic] plaid suit through which his great muscles bulged with the

intended effect on all who gazed upon him, and all gazed. A diamond, or a stone which had that appearance glittered in his scarlet tie. His shoes were polished to a state which made them throw off golden gleams whenever the light from a street lamp touched them. Whenever he spoke to a friend which was often – all the street seemed to know him – his two rows of pearly teeth gleamed from his seal-brown countenance. His hair was sleek under his grey derby.

In the second typescript, begun on January 15 and finished on February 5, 1926, the early description has been used as a preliminary sketch to which detail, color, motion, have been added:

Anatole Longfellow, alias the Scarlet Creeper, strutted aimfully down the east side of Seventh Avenue. He wore a tight-fitting suit of shepherd's plaid which thoroughly revealed his lithe, sinewy figure to all who gazed upon him, and all gazed. A great diamond, or a less valuable stone which aped a diamond, glistened in his fuschia [sic] cravat. His boots were polished to a state which made them throw off golden gleams whenever they encountered the light from a street lamp. The uppers of these shoes were dove-coloured suède and the buttons were pale blue. His hair was sleek under his grey derby. When he saluted a friend – he seemed to have a wide acquaintance – his two rows of pearly teeth gleamed from his seal-brown countenance.

In the third typescript, which is dated March 1, 1925, and from which type was set, the effects already created are condensed and shaped to the form in which they are found in print:

> Anatole Longfellow, alias the Scarlet Creeper, strutted aimfully down the east side of Seventh Avenue. He wore a tight-fitting suit of shepherd's plaid which thoroughly revealed his lithe, sinewy figure to all who gazed upon him, and all gazed. A great diamond, or some less valuable stone which aped a diamond, glistened in his fuchsia cravat. The uppers of his highly polished tan boots were dove-colored suède and the buttons were pale blue. His black hair was sleek under his straw hat, set at a jaunty angle. When he saluted a friend – and his acquaintanceship seemed to be wide – two rows of pearly teeth gleamed from his seal-brown countenance.

It was considered a wise precaution to have the galley proof read by a lawyer to avoid difficulty with the censor. The set of galleys shown in the exhibition was read and only a few passages required alteration before publication.

The author contributed a one-sentence blurb to the dust-jacket which indicates his opinions of the place of *Nigger Heaven* in his work: "Carl Van Vechten continues to act as historian of contemporary New York life, drawing a curious picture of a fascinating group hitherto neglected by writers of fiction."

The novel was attacked and hailed in the press. The *Independent* thought it "cheap French romance, colored light brown." "It is brilliant, but febrile and hysterical," declared the London *Saturday Review*, "a lurid side-light on the American scene." Yet the praise was louder than the

blame. Louis Kronenberger complimented Mr. Van Vechten in the *Literary Digest* for entering "a field both fertile
and unexplored . . . admirably suited to his talents." The
New York Evening Post called it "a novel full of torment, a
story stung out of life." The *Saturday Review of Literature*
spoke authoritatively: "From the viewpoint of style and
fullness 'Nigger Heaven' is Mr. Van Vechten's finest job.
In the last analysis it will be pointed to as a frontier work
of an enduring order."

Shortly after appearance of the novel a music publisher objected to the use in the text of the words of songs
he published. Mr. Van Vechten asked his friend, Mr. Langston Hughes, the Negro poet, to write him substitute lyrics,
of which the longest were "Harlem to duh bone" and
"Baby, lovin' baby." Cancel leaves carrying the new words
were first inserted in the sixth printing. The inscriptions by
the novelist and the poet on the flyleaf of the author's copy
of the sixth printing tell the story.

Nigger Heaven carried Mr. Van Vechten's fame all over
Europe. Between 1927 and 1933 the novel was translated
into Czech, Danish, Estonian, French, German, Hungarian,
Italian, Norwegian, Polish, Swedish. The Tauchnitz edition
was issued in 1928.

Of the hundreds of letters which Carl Van Vechten
received about *Nigger Heaven* none are more interesting
than those which came from his Negro friends. The title
shocked many of them before they understood it: the word
nigger grates on the ears of Negro and white alike. Other
aspects of the novel perturbed them, as Nora Holt, the
pianist and singer who suggested the character of Lasca Sar-

toris, wrote from France: "The cries of protest from the Harlemites reach me even in Paris."

When they read it, leaders in the Negro community immediately championed the novel. In one of the telegrams shown in the exhibition Paul Robeson praised "its absolute understanding and deep sympathy." In another Walter White protested the refusal by the *Courier* – on account of the title – to run an advertisement for the novel. The editor of *Opportunity*, Charles S. Johnson, wrote Mr. Van Vechten, "Your observation and honesty are to be thanked for this although you managed to get what many Negroes will regard as 'family secrets.' " The New York Public Library's 135th Street Branch – where Mary Love, the heroine, was a librarian – ran an evening's discussion of the book to which the author was invited. Charles W. Chesnutt, himself a novelist, wrote Mr. Van Vechten that the fate of the colored intellectual "is up to you and men like you."

Spider Boy

Like its predecessor, Carl Van Vechten's sixth novel was an excursion into a field new to him and then largely neglected by novelists – Hollywood. It might be argued that Hollywood would never have become itself without Broadway and was therefore almost an indigenous subject for the "historian of contemporary New York life." Mr. Van Vechten's attention had been aroused when Paramount had in 1925 turned *The Tattooed Countess* into *A Woman of the World*, starring Pola Negri. He himself had had no hand in the transformation. Yet he had not wasted the opportunities for observation afforded him by a first visit to the Coast in January 1927. In viewing the customs and frame of mind of moviedom with a satirical slant he was again starting a popular trend in *Spider Boy*.

The phenomenal success of *Nigger Heaven* prompted Alfred Knopf to the largest first printing which any of Mr. Van Vechten's novels had received. *Spider Boy, a scenario for a moving picture*, was published on August 15, 1928, in a large-paper edition of 295 copies (75 on Japan vellum and bound in red vellum and 220 on rag paper bound in blue paper boards) and a trade edition of 20,000 copies bound in pink cloth with gilt stamping. The English edition, which appeared the same year, carried the Knopf London imprint. On both sides of the Atlantic the dust-jacket displayed a drawing by Ronald McRae, in the manner of Ralph Barton.

The novel was dedicated to Blanche Knopf, who is the only friend to whom Mr. Van Vechten dedicated more than one book. Most appropriately Mr. Van Vechten's signature on the contract was witnessed on February 4, 1928, by Charlie Chaplin.

The first typescript of *Spider Boy* was begun on August 16 and completed on October 20, 1927. There are few ink corrections, noticeably fewer than in the typescripts of the preceding novels. The second typescript was begun the day after the first was finished and was concluded on December 28, 1927. It, too, is comparatively little worked over in pen and ink. The third typescript is dated January 27, 1928, carries a few final changes of word, and was used by the typesetters.

The proofs reveal one of those errors that throw off the entire arrangement of a book. In making up the pages in the second set of proofs, the printers followed through at the end of the first chapter, putting the beginning of the second chapter on the same page with the final paragraph of the first and so on throughout the rest of the volume. The result was a volume of 287 pages. When this was detected and altered so that each chapter began on a new page, the result was a volume of 297 pages.

Describing *Spider Boy* on the dust-jacket, Mr. Van Vechten referred to it as "his gayest novel." To many critics it was "riotously funny," as the *Boston Transcript* declared, or "as gay as a piece of music by Rodgers and Hart," according to the *New York Evening Post*. Though the *Spectator* felt "the humor may be too broad for many English readers," the London *Times* thought the "satire . . . pointed and extremely entertaining." The *New York Times* praised it as "a roistering farce of a mummer's wonderland," and the *New York Herald Tribune* found in it "the entire sociological, philosophical, financial and artistic conception of the motion pictures."

Spider Boy was translated into four foreign languages between 1929 and 1933: Danish, French, Italian, and Swedish. The French translation, by Maurice Rémon, ran in *La Revue Hebdomadaire* before book publication. The novel appeared in the Tauchnitz edition in 1928.

The curiosity that *Spider Boy* aroused in Hollywood is suggested by telegrams from two momentary stars in that impermanent firmament, Lois Moran and Carmel Myers. Miss Myers pointed out that gossip linked the heroine with

Pola Negri. Another star, Aileen Pringle, admitted to Mr. Van Vechten, "I hated it, I enjoyed it – I disliked it & ended by loving it." Gertrude Atherton, the novelist, though identified with San Francisco, wrote the author that the novel was "in spite of its deliberate exaggerations the best picture of Hollywood that has been done," and that she knew "because I spent nine months in that hell." The editor of *Photoplay*, James Quirk, declared, "In the guise of a novel you have done a good piece of reportorial work – a much better job than any of the hard hitting literary blacksmiths have done."

At the Metro-Goldwyn-Mayer studio in Hollywood, Carl Van Vechten posed with Aileen Pringle and the film director Mal St. Clair. The photograph shown in the exhibition was lent through the kindness of Mr. Gerald D. McDonald.

Parties

It was appropriate that an author who had been one of the spokesmen of the sophisticated side of the boom years should have been among the first to recognize the close of the era. The party was over on October 29, 1929, and two weeks later Carl Van Vechten began the novel which described some of the frenetic amusements of the past decade. The book was entitled *Parties*; it might as appropriately have been called hangovers, for the psychological tone of the story is one of disillusionment and philosophical bankruptcy. The pivotal character in *Parties* is David Westlake – between whom and F. Scott Fitzgerald a certain resemblance might be traced. At the morning cocktail party with which the story symbolically closes David gives the final toast: " 'We're here because we're here, and we should be extremely silly not to make the worst of it.' "

This speech is found in the very first typescript, which was begun on November 13, 1929, and completed on March 15, 1930. The typescript is corrected, though not heavily, in ink. The second typescript, unlike any other in the exhibition, was begun a month before the first was completed – on February 13, 1930 – and finished on March 25. Here Westlake's wife's name is Rilda instead of the original Gladys, a change which does not diminish her resemblance to Zelda Fitzgerald. The second draft also carries ink corrections. From the third, which is dated April 22, 1930, and marked with final changes, type was set.

No figure was more associated with the party atmosphere of the 1920s than Texas Guinan, who on April 29, 1930, witnessed Mr. Van Vechten's signature on the contract.

Parties was Mr. Van Vechten's last novel and last extensive piece of writing. It was as if he had come full circle to the point at which he had taken up the writing of fiction. The decade which had been host to his seven novels was over; he had said all he wanted to say about a way of living that was certainly for a time obsolete; he ceased to write fiction.

The pinch of the times was being felt when *Parties* appeared on August 15, 1930. It was published by Alfred Knopf in a large-paper edition of 250 copies bound in lemon yellow vellum and in a trade edition of 10,000 copies in lemon yellow cloth. Both bindings were ornamented in silver with a symbolic cupid treading grapes. The English edition, published in September 1930, bore the Knopf London imprint.

The binding of *Parties* was perhaps the most beautiful of all of Mr. Van Vechten's books. It was not achieved without trial and error. On display is a dummy with a binding that was discarded. The color of the cloth is more chartreuse than lemon. The silver cupid on the front cover is of a totally different design and lacks the frame of grape clusters; it is a smaller version of the figure found on the dust-jacket. The title of the book and the author's name are stamped on the spine in silver rather than in green. The top edges are stained wine red instead of green. The vignette on the title-page, similar to the discarded one on the front cover, is also printed in wine red instead of chartreuse.

The critics were not in the mood for the view of New York life reflected in the new novel. The bitter after-taste of the story was not immediately detected. True, Harry Hansen in the *New York World* called it "a gay sparkling novel about our times . . . of a society which is trying desperately to amuse itself." The London *Nation and Athenaeum* thought it "very clever" and the *Times* a "vivacious satire . . . a study of complete futility and abandonment . . . a clever study, but too complacent to be really clever."

Other critics, though they disliked it, did not find it complacent. "Tense and powerful and rather disgusting," declared George Daingerfield in the *Bookman*. The *New York Times* called the novel "unsavory and sniggering." Repelled by the drinking, the *Saturday Review of Literature* missed the point of view taken by the author: "Mr. Van Vechten has talents, of course – real talents. Is it not surprising that he uses them for books such as this one, which is flippant at best and occasionally a little – even more than a little – cheap?"

Armina Marshall, the actress, who shared the dedication of *Parties* with her husband, Lawrence Langner, the theatrical director, told Mr. Van Vechten in a letter of thanks that she found the novel "very amusing but at the same time a very tragic picture." Evelyn Waugh, whose novels were to delight readers of the 'thirties as Carl Van Vechten's had the 'twenties, wrote about *Parties*, "I feel that you have succeeded in doing such a lot that I was attempting in Vile Bodies." And Mr. S. Kato of Tokyo paid the novel a compliment never received by any of its predecessors. He requested permission to translate it into Japanese.

THE PHOTOGRAPHER

Carl Van Vechten's decision to write no more fiction could have only one result: that he would soon pour his creative energy into another form of expression. It was not until the second International Leica Exhibition of Photography in November 1935 that he revealed his new art – portrait photography. For the first time, he put his camera work on display. At once his portraits were hailed by Henry McBride in the *New York Sun*: "What is literature's loss is photography's gain. Quite distinctly Mr. Van Vechten is the Bronzino of this camera period. He works in the large, and with a boldness in design . . . that makes his work carry . . . emphatically. . . ."

For a quarter of a century Carl Van Vechten has continued to photograph, with enthusiasm and superb artistry, the theatrical, artistic, and literary personalities of two continents. He is happily still at work. The photograph of Theodore Dreiser shown in the exhibition was one of those in the second Leica Exhibition. That of William Faulkner was made on December 11, 1954.

A dozen of Mr. Van Vechten's portrait studies, taken over more than two decades, have been selected as representative of his penetrating camera-work and as illustrative of some of the personalities mentioned in this exhibition: Blanche Knopf and James Weldon Johnson (1932); Theodore Dreiser and Eugene O'Neill (1933); Gertrude Stein and a self-portrait (1934); James Branch Cabell and Alfred Knopf (1935); F. Scott Fitzgerald (1937); Sinclair Lewis (1938); Jean Cocteau (1949); and William Faulkner (1954).

THE FRIENDLY ADVOCATE

All through the years when he was producing his own essays and novels, and since then, Mr. Van Vechten has been instrumental in advancing the fortune of other writers and artists by writing about their work. Sometimes he contributed a paragraph or two for a dust-jacket. Frequently he produced an entire introduction for a book. By such generous acclaim he has sponsored the work of artists, playwrights, poets, and novelists, American and foreign, Negro and white. As the literary executor of Gertrude Stein, he has acted as general editor in the publication of the Yale University edition of her unpublished writings, of which four volumes have to date been issued.

On display is a selection of volumes for which he has written prefaces. These are *Fifty Drawings* by Alastair and *The Prince of Wales and Other Famous Americans* by Miguel Covarrubias, which contains a caricature of Mr. Van Vechten; *Sophie, a Comedy* by Philip Moeller; *The Lord of the Sea* by M. P. Shiel and *Prancing Nigger* by Ronald Firbank, two English novelists whose work he admired; *Born to Be* by Taylor Gordon, *The Weary Blues* by Langston Hughes; and *The Autobiography of an Ex-Coloured Man* by James Weldon Johnson; and Gertrude Stein's *Three Lives* and *Four Saints in Three Acts*.

This anniversary year has demonstrated the interest which Carl Van Vechten's work commands. A bibliography of his publications has been produced by Klaus W. Jonas and published by Alfred Knopf. Grace Zaring Stone, who also writes under the name of Ethel Vance, contributed an appreciative "preamble" entitled "Bouquet for Carlo." A study of his work in relation to his time – *Carl Van Vechten and the Twenties* by Edward Lueders – was published in May by the University of New Mexico Press.

Acknowledgments

"The Search for Sambir" by Richard D. Altick. From
The Scholar Adventurers by Richard D. Altick.
New York: The Macmillan Company, 1950, pp.
289–297. Reprinted by permission.

"A Doctor's Benefaction: The Berg Collection at
The New York Public Library" by John D. Gordan.
From *The Papers of the Bibliographical Society of America*
48 (Fourth Quarter, 1954), 303–314. Reprinted by
permission. This paper was read at the meeting of the
Society in New York, January 29, 1954.

"Charles Dickens: An Exhibition of Manuscripts,
Autograph Letters, and First Editions" by John D.
Gordan. New York: The New York Public Library,
1941.

"The Secret of Dickens' Memoranda" by John D.
Gordan. From *Bookman's Holiday: Notes and Studies
Written and Gathered in Tribute to Harry Miller Lydenberg*.
New York: The New York Public Library, 1943,
p. 188–195.

"*The Ghost* at Brede Place" by John D. Gordan.
From *Bulletin of The New York Public Library* 56
(December 1952), 591–595; reprinted by the Library
as a separate pamphlet, 1953.

This limited edition was composed by the Meriden-Stinehour Press in Monotype Bembo. Bembo is a copy of a roman cut by Francesco Griffo for the Venetian printer Aldus Manutius. It was first used in Cardinal Bembo's De Aetna, *1495, hence the name of the contemporary version, revived and adapted in 1929 by The Monotype Corporation. The paper used is Mohawk Superfine, with Curtis Flannel for the jacket. This book was designed by Sean Adams at The New York Public Library. The edition is limited to 1000 copies.*

◆